IN PRAISE OF POTEEN

IN PRAISE OF

POTEEN

JOHN
MCGUFFIN

APPLETREE

First published 1978 by
The Appletree Press Ltd,
6 Dublin Road Belfast BT2 7HL

Printed by
The Appletree Press Ltd

Cloth ISBN 0 904651 42 8
Paper ISBN 0 904651 36 3

CONTENTS

NOTE

ACKNOWLEDGEMENTS

Throughout the book I have spelt the word 'poitín.' This is the correct Irish spelling, the reason for the emasculated 'poteen' on the cover is my publisher's idea. I have also been asked by the same timorous gentleman to state categorically that the author and the publisher, in putting out this book in no way urge any reader to attempt to manufacture or purchase any poitín. To do so would be to break the law and you wouldn't want to do that, would you?

John McGuffin. Belfast 1977

This book could not have been written without the help of a large number of people, many of whom wish to remain anonymous. The list which follows is therefore unfortunately incomplete. For permission to reproduce photographs I am indebted to the Ulster Museum (Welch Collection), the National Library (Lawrence Collection), the N. Ireland Public Records Office, The Irish Times, the Cork Examiner, Colman Doyle, Joseph Dabney, Joe Graham, Mrs Mary Battle, and the Falls Hotel, Ennistymon. I would also like to record my gratitude to all the staff of the Public Library, Royal Avenue and the Linenhall Library for their usual cheerful assistance.

The police, in the shape of Inspector Jim Schofield of the RUC Museum, Enniskillen and Sgt Gregory Allen of the Garda Siochana, Dublin also generously provided photographic items. My thanks are due also to Michael McLaverty, Joseph Dabney and Father Gaughan for permission to reproduce some of their material. Finally, I owe a debt to the following which only they can know:-

Judith, Liam Begley, Terry Brown, Nial Keily, Ed Maloney, Frank Doherty, Harry Tipping, Joe Mulhern, Tony and Rosemary Canavan, Danny and Joan, Sean Lyons, Proinnsias MacArt, Deasun Breatnach, Kevin Danaher, Sean and Eamonn Stinson, Sean and Mary O'Reilly, Dan Nolan, Breandán Breatnach, Jack McCann, Bill and Jacqui Van Voris, Phyllis McAtackney, Ralf and Aine, Willie McKeever, Colin Durling, Norma Dawson, Kevin Boyle, Michael Farrell, 'Old Pa', Willie, Ben Lorimer, R.W. Grimshaw, Paddy 'Muldoon' and the faithful Igor, Uncle Porky John Molloy, Ben Carraher, and of course Willie Derra of Appletree.

This book is dedicated to the Bodger, all Lumberjacks and most poitin drinkers. Beidh lá geal gréine go fóill in Éirinn.

AN INTRODUCTION TO POITIN

'At Callyhill John Ennery has a seat; it lies at a small distance on ye left of ye great Road, in a fine sporting country; brush woods abound in ye part. There are neither inns nor Alehouses on Ys road, yet almost every house have for public Sale Aquavitae or Whiskey, which is greatly esteemed by ye Inhabitants, as a wholesome balsamic Diuretic; they take it here in common before their Meals. To make it the more agreeable they fill an iron pot with ys spirit, putting sugar, mint and butter and when it hath seethed for some time they fill their square cans which they call Meathers and this drink out then to each other. What is surprising they will drink it to Intoxication and are never sick after it neither doth it impair their health. An Irish doctor took on him, 30 years since, to give ye following ludicrous virtues of Aquavitae: i. dryeth ye breakins out on ye hands. ii. it killeth Fleshworms. iii. cureth ye scald of ye Hed. iv. keeps back old age. v. strengthens youth. vi. helpeth Dijestion. vii. cuteth phlegm. viii. casts off melancholy. ix. enlighteneth ye heart. x. expelleth ye gravel. xi. cureth ye dropsie. xii. healeth ye stranguary. xiii. quickeneth ye mind and spirits. xiv. wastes ye stones. xv. breaketh ye wind. xvi. keepeth ye hed from gidiness.'

This extract comes from Butler's Journey through Fermanagh in 1760. The drink described is poitin, which was the standard drink of the day. While not necessarily accepting the somewhat extravagant claims for it made by 'An Irish doctor', I feel that poitin has had a bad press, generally from those who have had a vested interest to abuse it — the licensed distillers, the Revenue Department and the Temperance groups — and this short book is an attempt to in some way redress the balance. It is not intended as the comprehensive work on the subject nor as a dull and scholarly tome, rather it is a miscellany of items and photographs concerned with the history of poitin up to the present day, for, as the reader may discover, the ancient art of poitin making flourishes yet.

A scoundrel who should have known better, one Brendan Behan, once said, 'no matter what anyone tells you about the fine old drop of the mountain dew, it stands to sense that a few old men sitting up in the back of a haggard in the mountains with milk churns and all sorts of improvised apparatus cannot hope to make good spirits.' Well, although Behan could certainly claim to be no stranger to the drink, it was the 'parliament whiskey' that did for him, and, as we shall see in the chapter about poitin making in jails, some of Brendan's experiences with 'the cratur' were somewhat bizarre. Similarly, in his book on Irish Whiskey F.B. McGuire writes sneeringly, 'poteen (sic) is poor stuff compared with the legal article, but it is cheap and will always have its advocates who will praise it with the zeal of eccentrics.' As one eccentric, who is not in the pay of the giant distillers, I write 'In Praise of Poitin'. And to those who make it and those who drink it, Slainte!

MICK McQUAIDES CABIN CONNEMARA

Mick McQuade's Cabin, Connemara,
c 1880. A typical poitín-maker's home.
(*Lawrence Collection, National Library of Ireland*)

CHAPTER 1 POITIN: A CHEQUERED PAST

Once upon a time the land belonged to everyone. The concept of various individuals 'owning' a particular piece of land and depriving others of its use was as laughable as anyone trying to claim that they owned the sun, the sky or the sea. Mankind and society 'evolved' however, and created for the benefit of the few, the State and the Law. The powerful and the greedy now claimed title to the common lands, the forests and the animals therein and the rivers and the fish therein. Those who protested were killed, driven off or dealt with by 'the Law'. By the 18th century in Ireland this process had been completed. 'Great' landlords 'owned' the land, the forest and the rivers. Peasants worked the land for a pittance while a few powerful and guilty men luxuriated in their castles, built by the labour of others, or led a life in 'society' in London. By then, people had been conditioned to think of this as natural. They were resigned. This was the 'normal order of things', or so the Church and the State taught them.

However, within the framework of bondage, providing you were not disloyal to the Crown or its agents, obeyed your Church leaders, didn't kill or steal and paid your tithes or rent, within reason, after coping with the almost fulltime task of survival, you could do what you liked. One of the things that the people of Ireland liked to do, and had done for centuries, for example, was to distil their own whiskey. The ingredients were easily obtainable as was the necessary equipment to manufacture it and so poitin was very popular. In some areas it was even estimated that one household in two had its own still, generally capable of distilling ten or twelve gallons at a time.

Kings and Queens like to fight wars however, to increase their power, influence, territory and wealth. In order to do this they have to raise armies, since few of them like to risk their own necks. And soldiers, churlish fellows, expect to get paid for risking their necks for someone's else's sake. True, you didn't have to pay them very much, but there were a lot of them and many kept getting killed and having to be replaced. So the Crown's advisors had to keep thinking up more and more ways to raise money. A wide range of essential goods were taxed, but, until the seventeenth century in Ireland at least, no one had had the barefaced audacity to try to tax people for manufacturing something for their own consumption. In 1661 however, a levy on spirits was introduced. In Ireland it was totally ignored. One hundred years later the Crown tried again. In the year 1760 the law was changed. Private distillation, unless licensed by the State, became a 'crime'. Overnight a large proportion of the Irish population became 'criminals'.

Prior to this there had been occasional pieces of legislation intended to get money from distillers, — for example, in 1731 an Act had been passed prohibiting distilling 'in the mountainous parts of the Kingdom remote from any market town' — but all had been completely ignored. Duty on Irish spirit, for the large scale manufacturer was only 4d a gallon at the end of the 17th century and by 1770 had only risen to 10d. Many distillers didn't even bother to pay this and its collection often represented more trouble than it was worth for the few revenue agents. The Crown however, got greedy. Revenue was again needed for wars and the spirit duty was raised. In 1775 it was 1s.2d. per gallon, by 1815 it was 6s.1½d. The revenue must be collected, the home distiller stopped.

This was to prove very difficult to do. High duty meant that poitin making, for so long generally made for personal consumption now became a lucrative proposition. Out in the hills of Ireland the challenge was taken up.

The illicit distiller's modus operandi changed very little over the years. His equipment was cheap and portable. So long as he had an isolated spot, running water and fuel, generally turf, he was ready to carry on his craft. A Dr. Donovan, a professor of chemistry, visited a poitin maker in the West of Ireland in 1830 and left us this description. It is almost certainly equally applicable to similar stills a century before or a century after this date.

'The distillery was a small thatched cabin, at one end was a large turf fire kindled on the ground and confined by a semi-circle of large stones. Resting on these stones, and over the fire, was a forty gallon tin vessel, which answered both for heating the water and the body of the still. The mash tun was a cask hooped with wood, at the bottom of which, next the chimb, (rim) was a hole plugged with tow. This vessel had no false bottom; in place of it the bottom was strewed with young heath; and over this a stratum of oat husks. Here the mash of hot water and ground malt was occasionally mixed for two hours; after which time the vent at the bottom was opened and the worts were allowed to filter through the stratum of oat husks and heath. The mashing with hot water on the grains was then repeated and the worts were again withdrawn. The two worts being mixed in another cask, some yeast added and the fermentation allowed to proceed until it fell spontaneously, which happened in about three days. It was now ready for distillation and was transferred into the body, which was capable of distilling a charge of forty gallons. A piece of soap weighing about two ounces was then thrown in to prevent its running foul; and the head, apparently a large tin pot with a tube at its side, was inserted into the rim of the body and luted (sealed) with paste made of oatmeal and water. A lateral tube was then luted into the worm, which was a copper tube of an inch and a half bore, coiled in a barrel for a flakestand (a worm tub). The tail of the worm where it emerged from the barrel was caulked with tow. The wash speedily came to the boil and water was thrown on to the fire; for at this period is the chief danger of boiling over. The spirit almost immediately came over; it was perfectly clear.'

Water in the worm tube was cooled by throwing buckets of cold water into the lower levels to force the warmer water at the top to overflow. Singlings were produced after about two hours and four such distillations made up a charge for producing poteen in a further distillation. Dr. Donovan reckoned it was very good quality stuff too. This particular distiller, like most of his contemporaries, used malt and oats, although at times raw corn was used to dilute the mixture. Nowadays, as we shall see in later chapters, many other staples are used, from molasses and treacle to rice and potatoes.

This seems to have been a fairly civilized still in operation, in stark contrast to that observed by Caesar Otway, who wrote in 1839: 'I observed two men working on a small lake island in Donegal, half naked, squalid, unhealthy looking creatures, with skins encrusted with filth, hair long, uncombed and matted, where vermin of all sorts seemed to quarter themselves and nidificate (build nests). The whole area of the island was one dunghill composed of fermenting grains; there were about twenty immense hogs either feeding or snoring on the floor that lay beneath them; and so alive with rats was the whole concern, that one of the boatmen compared them, in number and intrusiveness, to flocks of sparrows on the side of a shelling-hill adjourning a corn mill.' That was the local distillery.

Both these 'distilleries' were of course illegal, but up to the end of the 18th century the legal and illegal distiller existed side by side. For example, in the Bushmills/Coleraine area a distiller might be legal one day and illegal the next if the tax became prohibitive. The 1782 excise returns confirm that apart from Dublin itself the licensed distillers were all small time — 200/300 gallon stills being the norm — and they were scattered throughout the island. Each little village was likely to have its own distillery catering to local needs, since primitive road conditions tended to restrict sales.

In 1775 the duty on spirit was raised from 10d to 1s.2d. This encouraged quite a few distillers to 'go illegal', but five years later came a much more serious incentive. The still license duty was imposed as the minimum spirit duty. This meant that in order to operate legally the small distiller had to manufacture a minimum number of gallons per week. In many cases the quota was far too high for the small man and he couldn't hope to sell that amount weekly, but, whether he did or not, or whether he produced that quantity or not, he was still taxed as if he had. Of course falsified returns and bribery of revenue officers became commonplace, but some small distillers tried to keep up and expand their sales. Their position was worsened however when the Government passed new regulations insisting that the distiller charge his still twice a week, and then, by the turn of the century, once a day. This was the final straw for many and it forced literally hundreds of relatively law abiding distillers into illicit distillation. This can easily be seen from some examples of licensed stills;

	1782	1796
Co Cavan	39	2
Co Armagh	74	9
Co Derry	19	0
Strabane	74	0

One important result of this was that the quality of legal (or 'parliament whiskey' as it was called) declined as distilleries were forced to work faster and faster. The poitin maker on the other hand could work at the old time honoured pace and so produce a markedly superior product. Caesar Otway, writing in 1839 proclaimed that 'to every Irishman poitin is superior in sweetness, salubriety and gusto, to all that machinery, science and capital can produce in the legalized way.' In 1823 an official Government report admitted that 'in Belfast poitin is expensive (three times the price it was in Derry) but it is consumed principally by the better classes where price is no consequence but quality is everything'. A Limerick legal distiller added ,' except for the dignitaries of the Church, the officers of the Army and the magistrates of the county, there is not anyone who cares a farthing about poitin here'. There is no accompanying evidence to show that the inhabitants of these areas all took the pledge overnight nor that drink was suddenly imported in vast quantities and the obvious explanation is that they just continued to distil without telling the tax man about it. In contrast to these areas in the North, in the South, where transport was better and law enforcement more practical, many small distilleries just collapsed, leaving a few who were capable of expanding and streamlining production.

Kilbeggan Distillery. In the early 19th century nearly every small town in Ireland had its own distillery. Most like this one were water powered. The barrels on the left were the standard whiskey kegs. (Lawrence Collection, National Library of Ireland)

Also, in 1825 Blake reports that 'the grand jury of a Western town retain the right to drink poitin at their common table, so much did its members prefer it to the lawful spirit.' These sentiments prevailed for quite some time. J. Bateman, in the 'Excise Officers Manual' of 1865 says that 'the preference was so strong in favour of illicit whiskey that when it was sold at an excise auction it fetched nearly double the price of the legally distilled article.'

The decades up to 1823 can be seen as the golden age of poitin. It was a better product than the rushed parliament whiskey, it was far cheaper to produce and the risks run, particularly in remote areas, were pretty negligible. It was popular, hardly surprisingly. In 1823 a Dublin distiller (legal) claimed that 'poitin accounts for a half if not two thirds of all spirit sales in Ireland.' There are plenty of reports to show that not only was it popular, but also widely available. City distillers complained vigorously that 'illicit spirits are sold openly in the streets of Dublin itself, as openly as you would sell a loaf of bread in London.' The same story was heard from Belfast, Armagh and New Ross, all areas which produced little poitin themselves but where there was a steady market for 'the stuff'. And, given the demand, there were men and women ready to take the risks to fulfil it. These were the 'cadgers', professional poitin distributors who travelled the length and breadth of the country filling orders. Harassed and harried by the revenue police (of whom more later) they seem to have thrived, aided and abetted by a legion of spies, subagents and bribed policemen.

In Derry around 1800 the cadgers were so confident that the poitin was brought to town from Inishowen, one of the most famous poitin centres, in open tubs on donkeys. Later, with the revenue police much thicker on the ground it was carried in tin cases on men's backs. The Government report of 1823 indignantly reports, 'some women have pockets made of tin, and a breast and a half moon that goes before them, and, with a cloak around them they will walk with six gallons and it shall not be perceived.' The ubiquitous Caesar Otway, this time touring in Connaught, reported that a local distiller had ordered from a tinker 'a tin vessel with the head and body the shape of a woman which he dressed to resemble his wife' and so rode to market with the poitin pillion behind him. Local folklore told of poitin being moved about in everything from small turf carts to coffins at fake funerals.

1823 was to see a change in the law to the advantage of the legal spirit distiller. MPs like H.R. Pakenham had long been complaining about the system. 'I confess I am at a loss for a proper term to apply to a system that offers to supply the community with a bad article at an expensive rate and then endeavours to force consumption of the stuff rendered pernicious by their own regulation' he said. Other distillers agreed, cursing what they called 'the tyranny of speed' which forced them to compete on very unfavourable terms with the poitin maker, turning out an inferior product at an inflated price. The protests finally paid off however, and, in 1823, the licensed distillers were now allowed to take more time to distil. Further representations were at once made that 'now the Government effectively tackle the problem of illicit distillation.' But do not shed too many tears for the plight of the 'poor honest distiller' as many called themselves. Few were poor and even fewer honest. They might complain bitterly about the amount of duty they were expected to pay, but they rarely paid it in full. The official revenue inquiry of the time claimed that 'the distillers can afford to bribe largely and they do so to an incredible extent. The formidable duties tempt them to bribe at such a high rate, as no virtue yet found in an excise man can withstand'. So complex were the actual mechanisms of collecting the excise on spirits that it placed the distillers 'so much in the power of the officers as necessarily to lead to undue intimacy between them.' In other words, corruption abounded.

Thus from 1823 the lot of the licensed distiller improved and the poitin maker came under increasing attack. He had other enemies apart from the law too; there was, for instance, the weather. The price of poitin actually fell from 8s a gallon to 4s a gallon from 1823 to 1835, mainly due to the weather. The reason for this was simple. Good weather meant a good crop of barley. The farmers would have a surplus and so would sell at least half of it locally to the poitin makers. Obviously up to a point this was desirable from his point of view, but too good a crop and the area would be flooded with poitin and so the price would fall. Still, even at a low price there was money to be made. In rural areas most families were large and there was a surplus of labour. Many would be casual and seasonal poitin makers. One could rent or buy a still cheaply. For example, in 1834, travelling tinkers were selling tin stills with copper worms, capable of holding 50 - 60 gallons for about £1 in Mayo and Galway and £2 in Derry. The really fastidious craftsman could buy a copper still and worm, plus flax seed casks for fermenting and a sugar hogshead for use as a mash tun for about £6. In 1834 a Derry distiller gave the revenue inquiry his estimate of the poitin maker's costs once he had his still:

'18 stone of oats @ 7d a stone = £1.1s. From that he will get just over 8 gallons which he can easily sell at between 5 and 6 shillings a gallon. Moreover, he can sell the singlings for cattle food thus making about 150% profit.'

Of course, if the poitin travelled it would be sold for more — at that time it was fetching 10 - 12 shillings a gallon in Belfast — but it was the cadger who took the risks and the extra profit.

In 1854 the Select Committee on Illicit Distillation produced the following expenses sheet for the poitin maker:

Expenditure			*Income*		
40 stone oats	£4	2s 6d	17 gallons of spirit	£5	19s
Hire of still		1s 6d	plus sale of refuse		12s
Fuel		6d		£6	11s
Yeast		1s 6d			
	£4	6s 0d			

Profit £2 5s 0d

A revenue officer at the enquiry claimed that 'the average poitin maker can clear 3s a gallon profit'. This wasn't as good as in his father's day. Chichester reckoned that in 1818 after 'deducting all their losses, expenses and risks, together with the bribes paid to the revenue officers, the poitin maker makes £1 for each day he works.' There were other drawbacks however, as Chichester mentions that 'every idle blackguard in the locality would think it neighbourly to drop in for a taste without dreaming to pay for the privilege.' Despite these occupational hazards then, and taking into account the widely fluctuating prices, poitin making was a profitable business, and for some small peasant farmers a very necessary supplement to their precarious income.

This brings us to the attitude of the landlords towards poitin. Why did they not try harder to stamp out this illegal trade? Some did, averring that 'cheap spirit does make the peasants idle, careless and impertinent. T'is but a short step from them drinking poitin to talking politicks', while a Donegal rector was of the opinion that poitin making tended 'to promote dissipation, perjury, rebellion, revenge and murder.' This was a view held too by the Earl of Kingston, who effectively stopped illicit distillation in much of Co. Cork for a time by putting a clause in his tenants lease to the effect that a conviction for poitin making would be automatic grounds for eviction. These men were an exception however. Many landlords realized that their chances of getting the rent paid promptly and in full depended upon the extra revenue poitin brought in. The peasant's life was hard and difficult. He lived at subsistence level for the most part. In Sligo for example the local rector is quoted by Mason as saying; 'Even if distilling were made a felony punishable by death the poor of my parish would not desist since they had no other means of paying their rents and might as well hang as starve.' The Excise Commissioners themselves claimed in 1834 that many 'would almost as soon be in prison during the winter season as at their own cabins; they fare much better ... they have a sufficency of potatoes, oatmeal and milk and have good warm bedding. They feel no disgrace at being in prison and believe friends will support their families'. While this, I am sure, is unduly complimentary to the Irish prison service of the day, it is true that prison, for the illicit distiller was frequently dismissed as an 'occupational hazard'.

Certainly going to prison for poitin making carried no stigma. Few landlords would think the worse of a tenant whom he knew to be paying his rent with the profits he derived from poitin. Indeed, if the Excise Commisioners are to be believed some Galway landlords at times accepted poitin in lieu of rent money and had been heard to boast 'if there were 50,000 troops they would not be able to put it down.' Indeed in Leitrim a landlord's agent was to claim to the Commissioners 'private distillation is the *only* means they have to pay the rent.' Nor were all the clergy opposed to poitin. B.W. Noel claimed in 1836 that there was a friar on Achill Island who made most of his living from blessing illicit stills, while Caesar Otway averred that 'very many clergy only get their tithes as a result of illicit distillation.' Indeed, he alleged, in Erris, in 1841 there existed a chapel with part of it converted into a distillery.

'A house contrived a double debt to pay,
A still by night, a place of prayer by day.'
Thus giving a new meaning to the old hymn, 'Oft in the stilly night?' And so, with so many 'respectable' elements tolerating if not actively supporting illicit distillation it was often difficult to get judges or juries to convict the poitin maker. Why then, with poitin so profitable and socially acceptable did it decline so rapidly in the late 19th century and why did the craft exist in restricted areas of Ireland? There are several reasons.

But first, a brief look at illicit distillation in Scotland. This is not as irrelevant as it might appear. Just as in Ireland, in Scotland illicit distillation flourished. In 1820 there were about 4,000 convictions for poitin making, and it should always be remembered that the number of convictions only represented the tip of the iceberg. And yet, within a decade all this had changed, illicit distillation had been virtually wiped out in Scotland. What had happened was that leaders of the gentry, with the Duke of Gordon particularly active, had offered the Government a deal behind the backs of their tenantry. If the Government would lower dramatically the duty on whisky, they would stop the manufacture of poitin by their tenants; with poitin wiped out, the Government would get more revenue despite the lower duty and the gentry could make profits out of the new crop of distilleries. The bargain was sealed. In 1823 the Government cut the duty on Scotch whisky from 6s 2d to 2s 4¾d. Within ten years poitin making had virtually died out in the Highlands and the Lowlands.

Because they chose, for various reasons not to apply the same tactics in Ireland poitin enjoyed a much longer run. If we examine the court records we can even compile a 'top ten' of the poitin counties. Here for example is the 1816 top ten , based on the number of townland fines imposed upon each barony

Typical eviction scene, c 1880. The Land League was founded by Michael Davitt to oppose the bloodsucking cruelty of absentee landlords. Their weapons included the boycott, and on occasion, physical force, hence the presence of armed soldiers. (Lawrence Collection, National Library of Ireland)

Tourists buying poitín (?) (Lawrence Collection, National Library of Ireland)

in the counties by the courts. (Townland fines are dealt with in the next chapter).

1.	Co Donegal	531	6.	Co Clare	83
2.	Co Tyrone	151	7.	Co Leitrim	74
3.	Co Derry	127	8.	Co Antrim	55
4.	Co Mayo	108	9.	Co Sligo	54
5.	Co Galway	86		Co Tipperary	

In effect, these were the poitin counties. Relatively the others didn't count. Small time illicit distillation may have gone on in other counties but not on such a scale as to worry the authorities. Of course, partisans of each county can claim that the reason why their county wasn't higher up the list of 'notoriety' was incompetent law enforcement, greater skill in concealment on the part of the poitin makers, remoteness of the locations or more corrupt and bribable revenue men. All these points need to be considered, but when a glance at the records for nearly a century shows roughly the same order, we can take it that Co Donegal, Co Derry, Co Tyrone and Co Mayo were what the Revenue Commissioners called 'the most infected areas.'

The reasons for this are not hard to discern. Remoteness was, and still is a priceless asset for the poitin maker. Poor roads and lack of transportation were to his advantage. In these areas poitin was established when there was little competition and people grew to prize it so much that the parliament whiskey, when it became more widely available, was scorned by most people in these areas. They prefered the 'smoky' taste of the malt whiskey to the rough taste of the grain whiskey. Cost was, of course another major factor in these poorer areas. In the Midlands and the South where transport and detection was much easier poitin making died out fairly early in the century. Then too there was the competition of porter, virtually unknown in the far North West but very popular in Dublin and Cork.

One of the few mysteries indeed is why West Cork and Kerry were never renowned for poitin making. Some, of course, was made, but apparently very little and yet, like the North-West they too were remote, had plenty of running water and turf and, if necessary, an available market in Cork City. Various explanations none of them totally satisfactory, have been put forward, — the ground was under pasturage to produce butter, grain was harder to get, legal distilling was more efficient because of the availability of coal — but, whatever the real explanation, it is true to say that by 1823 poitin making was restricted to the ten counties previously mentioned. In the South and East the licensed distiller, often bribing his way out of paying the full tax, expanded and consolidated. He may have added to his rising profits by distilling a little extra spirit on the side, but, by and large, it was in his interests to become 'respectable' and law abiding. On the other hand, the poorer peasant in the far West or North was economically almost forced into illegality.

Despite the Act of 1823 poitin making flourished, at least up until the famine years. Thereafter it declined, albeit not as rapidly as some would have us believe. What were the reasons for this? Changes in enforcement and better communications had a part to play as we shall see in the next chapter, but there were other reasons. In some areas the Church played a major role in the fight against poitin. After 1838 the temperance campaign of Father Matthew (1790-1856) was effective. Amongst the grandiose claims made for the man was one that he administered more than 5,000,000 pledges — well over half the adult population — during a six year campaign, and, that thanks to him 20,000 bankrupt publicans had to flee the country while spirit revenue dropped from £1,435,000 in 1839 to £852,000 in 1844. These figures almost certainly owe more to the famine than to the wondrous powers of this meddling priest however. The decimation of the population through famine, death and enforced emigration would, to say the least, hit poitin production. If a man is threatened with death to himself and his family by the potato blight he isn't going to risk using the little grain he may have for distillation. After the worst of the famine years poitin making was still carried on of course, though on a lower scale. Le Fanu in his travels in the 1890s tells of regular and blatant poitin making in Co Donegal in the month of July, when all the police were away to put down the annual riots in Derry. It was here too that the Church interfered again. In 1892 Dr. John O'Doherty, Catholic Bishop of Derry (his diocese also took in Inishowen) made the distilling of poitin a reserved sin and soon after in Co Donegal, Co Fermanagh and Co Tyrone the Bishops followed suit. (A reserved sin means that only the bishop and not an ordinary confessor can give absolution for this 'sin'). As a result of these authoritarian busybodies the Congested District Board in 1909 was pleased to report that 'a drop of poitin could scarce be found in Tyrconnell (Donegal)'. An exaggeration, but not a grotesque one.

Land reform played its part as well in the eclipse of poitin. The Royal Commission of 1906 smugly pointed out that 'once a man becomes the owner of land he drinks far less.' Certainly overall consumption of spirits fell between 1857 and 1922 as far as we can tell from the available figures. Prior to the campaign of the Land League and the subsequent land reform measures the peasant's lot had often been so miserable that poitin drinking had often been his only release from his troubles. It was cheap, easy to make and, for a time, profitable. Small wonder that he indulged himself. Once he owned a small piece of land however, the threat of prison became a much more serious proposition.

Then too, as the quality of parliament whiskey steadily improved, the quality of much of the poitin declined due to the use of alien and inferior materials. At the same time there was an increase in the consumption of porter and beer as it became more widely available in the outlying areas. Thus, for a variety of reasons poitin making declined in the latter half of the 19th century. But the art never died out and, as we shall see, there are still artists who kept the old craft alive.

RUC seizure, Co Derry, c 1925. (RUC Enniskillen)

CHAPTER 2   POITIN AND THE LAW

Living, as he or she tended to do, in the more remote parts of the country many poitin makers had little to fear from the excise man. In the 18th century there was no organized police force and the excise men could not pursue the illicit distiller without the aid of a military escort. The military themselves were often not too keen on this duty, for the poitin makers were frequently armed and organized in gangs. G. E. Howard, himself an excise man wrote in 1776 that 'revenue officers are frequently assaulted, wounded and sometimes killed in the execution of their duty and often receive little assistance to which they are entitled from the military'. Occasionally raids were successful, for instance the Dublin Annual Register for 1778 reports the following: Limerick. Feb. 25th.

'On the 20th inst John Downes Esquire, Inspector of Excise, accompanied by some other civil officers and a detachment of the 27th regiment with two field pieces, proceeded to attack the castle of Ognolly in which has been carried on for some years an immense distillery in open defiance of the laws; but on the first appearance of the military force the castle surrendered without the least resistance. In it was found one of the most compleat distilleries in the Kingdom, which they totally destroyed'.

All raids were not so bloodless. In County Armagh — 'bandit country' as someone called it — in 1797 several militia men on revenue duty were killed in a clash with 'a mob'. After this a decision was taken not to send any more parties of soldiers to assist the revenue men, but this was revoked three years later and the searches began again. It was said that to permit a seizure of one's poitin was an affront to a Donegal man. In Inishowen, where, according to an official Government report of 1824 'the people are smugglers and distillers from the cradle', gangs of 60 or 80 men, 'so ferocious they needed an army to defeat them' often engaged the army and revenue men. In 1819 a force of 140 infantry and 40 cavalry were repulsed and forced to flee by the people of Buncrana and Culdaff who were reported to be 'armed and openly contemptuous of the authorities'. In County Mayo by Erris nearly 200 distillers were openly at work according to the Government, guarded by a large crowd of 'dissolute youth'. Their stills were well protected, bounded as they were by mountains and the sea and approachable only through two easily guarded passes. In 1815 the Government had tried to take issue with such flagrant criminal activity and had dispatched a group of excise men with 30 soldiers to make arrests. But the distillers, trained it was said by a deserter from the army, were ready for them and repulsed them after permitting a token amount of singlings to be seized.

In Donegal similar engagements were not uncommon. Gamble, in his 'Views of Society and Manners in the North of Ireland' records how 'flying mountaineers used to leave trails of poitin scattered behind them which the pursuing soldiers used to attack and greedily swallow'. As a result, since obviously rotgut would be left behind voluntarily, 'the English militia tumbled down senseless on the heath until they had slept themselves sober'. They were the lucky ones! The Londonderry Journal of the time reports that revenue officers were not infrequently carried off 'by the banditti' in sacks and forced to work the stills. Between 1808 and 1818 the Journal records at least half a dozen deaths of revenue men and distillers. For example, a private in the Dublin militia was killed near Buncrana when 'ferociously assailed by stones'. Six men of the North Hampshires were disarmed and beaten up near Stranorlar, while their officer was fatally wounded, and on at least three occasions excise men had to be acquitted of killing illicit distillers. Today's custom officer is well off by comparison.

In 1783 the Government had imposed a £20 fine on a county or a town where any 'still, alembic (an old piece of distilling apparatus) or blackpot' was found. Following much protest the area involved was reduced, but this fine, which in effect went on the rates caused much distress. It meant that if part of a still was found on your little bit of land you were liable for a very heavy fine. Naturally this led to the poitin maker hiding his equipment on his neighbour's land. Thus many innocent people were ruined and often had to flee, being unable to pay the fines incurred. The Erne Packet of 1809 has a letter which gives a succinct eye-witness account:

'I observed the tenants of one townland driving their cattle wildly behind the hills, the women running from hut to hut sympathising with one another, the children trembling and other indications of terror and alarm. Reason — the townland had incurred a still fine!'

Since bounties were paid for information leading to the capture of a still, corruption and trickery were commonplace. An easy way to pay off a grievance or settle an old score was to plant part of a still on your enemy's land and then get the revenue men in.

Model still, used to train police recruits.
(RUC Enniskillen)

Left:
'I'm only doing my job.' Lowly RIC man,
c 1890. (Lawrence Collection, National
Library of Ireland)

This photograph was taken by W.A. Green
in 1926 on the Inishowen peninsula, where
the government claimed that 'the people
are smugglers and distillers from the
cradle.' The worm is hidden in the barrel of
water on the left. In this the steam from the
pot condenses into poteen. (Ulster Folk
Museum)

Caught in the act. Posed police photographs, c 1890. (Lawrence Collection, National Library of Ireland)

Informers became rife and were in their turn harshly dealt with. The Ennis Chronicle of 1792 for example relates how one such informer in Clare had 'one of his ears with part of his cheek cut off' and his body and head 'shockingly battered and lacerated'. Moreover, since only part of a still had to be found for a reward to be granted the greedy informer could break up a still into five or six parts and hide them about the place, thus guaranteeing more reward for himself and more hatred for the gauger or revenue man.

The aim of townland fining had been to force landlords to lend their support to eradicating illicit distillation, but this doesn't seem to have worked. Certainly some landlords, like the Earl of Kingston, previously mentioned, did act, but the vast majority seem to have joined in the game of 'musical stills,' frantically shifting stills from one townland to another before the gaugers struck. At first the fine was £60 for each offence — a huge sum in the late 18th century — but this was soon reduced to £25 for a first offence, £40 for a second and £60 for the third. Failure to pay could result in confiscation of property — hence the efforts of the peasants mentioned in the Erne Packet to move their cattle on to a friendly neighbour's land — or jail. Originally the collection of the townland fine was the responsibility of officers appointed specifically for that task by the grand juries, but, because they proved totally incompetent and corrupt their duties were soon taken over by the Board of Excise in 1815. Since the excise men received a bonus in the form of half the townland fine for themselves they clearly had a vested interest in discovering stills but yet they appear to have been very conscious of not wanting to kill the goose that laid the golden egg, and so they often restricted themselves to token seizures with occasional bonuses in order not to make themselves redundant.

In the poorest poitin areas, such as Donegal, Leitrim and Sligo the townland fines caused much real hardship. Confiscation of livestock was a disaster from which few small peasant farmers could recover: many were jailed, thus becoming a further burden on the parish and many were forced to flee, thus impoverishing the land and the people and not even raising any more money for the Government. In addition to the hostility felt for the revenue man by the peasant and the landlord there was the attitude of the military. As mentioned before, they had never been happy about revenue duty, officers often concerned lest their men drank all the poitin they discovered, an obvious temptation for the ill-paid and ill-treated foot soldier, to say nothing of them getting killed or maimed and so, in 1817 commanding oficers issued orders which effectively meant that their men, detailed from on high for revenue duty, would be of no use whatsoever to the excisemen. Henceforth soldiers were not to be allowed to make seizures themselves and had to remain within sight of the excisemen at all times. This was obeyed to such a ludicrous extent that Morewood reports seeing a group of excisemen trying to batter down a stout door, watched by a party of soldiers while sweating gangs of poitin makers formed lines to pass stills and poitin out the back door and up over the hill.

Since 1787 there had been, in addition to the revenue men, small bands of bounty hunters who had had private contracts with the excise to track down stills. They had had some success for example in Co. Leitrim where a rogue, one Patrick Carter, had led them. So in 1818 the Board of Excise, fed up with the lack of military assistance being accorded them, decided to expand the operations of the bounty hunters. The various small bands were amalgamated and augmented and came to be known as the Revenue police. They were armed, received regular pay in addition to any bounties they might get and had two permanent stations, at Ballina and Sligo.

They were financed directly by the Board of Excise and cost some £20,000 per annum in 1820, rising to £35,000 in 1833. It was hoped that they would be less corrupt than their predecessors, though why anyone was rash enough to suppose any such thing is a mystery. As one witness was to point out to the apparently dullwitted inquiry board later, to have been really efficient would have been to make oneself redundant and out of a soft job. Initially there were some 1,000 men in the force and they were given considerable powers. Colonel William Brereton was later to tell the inquiry that 'the law has given to this force powers stronger and more summary than to any other armed force of the Empire.' They could enter and search without a warrant, destroy stills and pour away the contents (or drink it) and use 'such force as they felt necessary' to achieve this. In the event of civilians getting killed or seriously wounded in the course of such a raid, as quite often happened, the Revenue police involved were automatically allowed bail and for a defence could simply plead the Act of 7 & 8 Geo 4 c 53. Yet despite such draconian powers they seem to have been totally ineffective. The 1820s were to see poitin making on the increase as tax on parliament whiskey rose.

One reason why they were ineffective was lack of co-ordination. Moreover they kept virtually no records and did very little actual work. Thomas Drummond, later to become Under-secretary of Ireland observed them in 'action' on several occasions between 1826 and 1828 and was not impressed. 'What I saw gave me no very favourable opinion of the proceedings', he wrote. 'It is difficult to conceive anything more ridiculous than half a dozen men, very conspicuous on account of their dress, viz white cross-belts over green uniform,

strolling out of town at noonday on such an expedition. They might as well send a messenger to give notice of their approach.'

Gloomily, Government report after report told of their failure to stamp out 'the pernicious spread of poitin'. They complained about lack of assistance from the other forces of 'law and order', namely the constabulary and the coastguard. Why wouldn't they assist the Revenue police? was the perennial cry. The answer was quite simple. The local coastguard and constable wanted a quiet life. He had to live in the area and couldn't move on like the Revenue man. Why on earth should he side with the men generally detested by at least 90% of the population with whom he lived and worked? Besides, he probably enjoyed a drop of poitin as much as the next man. So criticisms of the Revenue police mounted but the Board of Excise stubbornly resisted attempts to disband the force. They refused to consider the obvious remedy which was working in Scotland, that of decreasing the duty on parliament whiskey to take the profit out of poitin; instead they decided to reorganize the force.

The task was entrusted to Colonel William Brereton, a former army officer, who was appointed Inspector-General of Excise in 1836.

Brereton believed in a policy of root and branch. Two thirds of the existing force were sacked on the spot. A training depot was set up in Dublin for new recruits, who had to be single men, under 25 years of age and able to read and write. They got 1s 3d per day, lived in barracks, were forbidden to 'consort with the local people', and got a new suit of clothes every year as well as rewards for seizures of stills.

We'll get a few bob for this lot, lads.' Garda celebrate. (T. W. Battle)

Still head & Worm with worts and vessels	£3 3s
Still & head	£2 2s
Pot ale or worts & vessels	£1 1s
Simple still	10s
Head or worm	5s

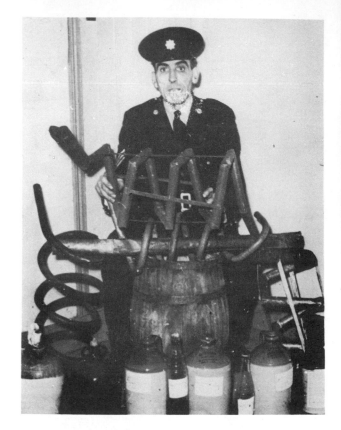

Officers got up to 6s 6d a day and had to be 'sons of gentlemen'. Brereton was a personal friend of Colonel McGregor, the Inspector-General of the constabulary and relations between the two forces improved, though apparently the coastguards were still unco-operative. To counteract this Brereton prevailed upon the Commissioners to purchase a boat and for several years the cutter was to become the scourge of the small islands off Sligo, Leitrim and Donegal where the poitin maker had for long enjoyed virtual immunity.

Brereton was a tough disciplinarian. His men were expected to march two hundred miles a week seeking out illicit spirit and to keep records, known as 'still-bills' of every day's work. By now they were costing £45,000 a year yet their success was only partial. When they saturated the most notorious counties with men it is true that the rate of poitin making declined, but only to increase in the neighbouring counties and once they withdrew the area was soon 'infected' again. The disposition of the police groups in 1854 shows that poitin making was still a major problem and that the same areas were still the most troublesome:

Munster (Clare, Tipperary) — 4 parties.

Leinster (Longford, Dublin) — 5 parties.

Connaught (Galway, Sligo, Mayo, Leitrim) — 29 parties.

Ulster (Donegal, Cavan, Tyrone, Fermanagh, Derry, Monaghan) — 34 parties.

And the statistics of prosecutions and discoveries indicate that although progress had been made, the force was not really effective. The famine of course contributed, in a devastating way, to a decrease in the amount of poitin being made but the Government wasn't satisfied and again began to think of scrapping the revenue police. A select Committee in 1854 recommended against any such action but, surprisingly they were overruled and in 1857 Brereton's force was disbanded. Henceforth revenue duties were to be undertaken by the constabulary.

Virtually no one liked the new plan, least of all the constabulary. Previously they had reluctantly

moved against large numbers of shebeens and so incurred the wrath of the local drinkers. Shebeens hadn't been too hard to find; those on the edge of town used to advertise by hanging turf outside. They would generally keep a little parliament whiskey for show and a lot more poitin for consumption. (It should be remembered that they were the only drinking places for local constables as well). Others too were unhappy. An M.P. claimed in the House of Commons that 'the suspicion existed that if the police found poitin they would drink it instead of destroying it.'

Gradually, in the wake of the famine, as parliament whiskey became relatively cheaper and more available and barley in scarcer supply, poitin making began to decline. Land reform played its part in this as we have seen, and it was only in the truly remote areas that the old craft continued. The pressure was taken off the police as poitin was felt to be less of a threat to the economy and they were able to turn a blind eye to it. But it still continued to be made almost openly in some parts. The reward system still continued and was still abused. It was after all a handy way for the poorly paid rural constable to

29

augment his pay. As late as 1901, when rewards were totalling some £3,000 a year, the Chief Secretary for Ireland admitted that there were 'many abuses' and in 1902 an Irish MP alleged that the same still had been seized 200 times. Faked seizures like this didn't harm the local people and benefitted the RIC man, while apparently mollifying the Revenue department in Dublin. That poitin making was blatantly condoned by the police as late as 1918 is shown in the following light hearted account of a raid on Inismurray Island, off the coast of Leitrim by Constable Jeremiah Mee and his colleagues. The extract comes from Mee's Memoirs, (Anvil Press:)

POTEEN HUNTING AT INISMURRAY ISLAND

'A few days after my arrival in Grange I was ordered to accompany Sergeant Connolly and Constable Clarke to Inismurray Island on revenue duty, that is, "poteen hunting". I was supplied with an official life-belt. This was a kind of waistcoat, made of squares of cork about the size of half bricks which were threaded together with thin wire. It was fitted under the police tunic and gave the wearer an ungainly appearance.

Until then I had never been in a boat except on Lough Gill, where I was always within easy reach of one of the islands, and safety. It was therefore with some misgivings that I donned the cork waistcoat which was to act as my life-belt while crossing the five miles of very rough sea which extended between the mainland and Inismurray. Besides the life-belts, the sergeant and Constable Clarke and myself were equipped with long, pointed steel rods which were to be used for probing hay and corn stacks, and shingle along the strand, in our search for illicit stills.

At Streedagh Point a small boat manned by two hefty Mullaghmore fishermen was waiting for us. The fishermen wore sea-faring clothes and had their caps, with the peaks turned back, pulled well down over their foreheads the better to withstand the stiff breezes coming in from the Atlantic. As there was no proper pier and the water was shallow for several yards out from the shore the boat was at anchor in fairly deep water. With their pants folded well above their knees the two fishermen advanced from the boat to meet us. On reaching the strand, after a peremptory greeting, they turned their backs on the sergeant and Clarke who got up on the fishermen's backs and were carried high and dry to the little boat. The two R.I.C. men took this as a matter of course and the sergeant did not even smile as I sat on the shore laughing at the unusual sight. One of the boatmen returned when I, too, got up on his back and never in my life did I feel less like a policeman.

The sea was choppy, as the boatmen euphemistically put it, and my cork waistcoat did not prevent my heart thumping as the little boat ploughed through mountainous seas. To add to my discomfort the boatmen regaled us with stories of lucky escapes which they had from sharks while out fishing for herring around Inismurray Island. It seems that the fishermen were guided to the herring shoals by the presence of hundreds of seagulls hovering over them. The sharks, too, kept close to the herring shoals and from time to time made circuits at great speed around the fish. If the nets are set while the shark is making his circuit he is liable to be caught in it, and as he pulls on it the boat can be swamped unless the fishermen are quick enough to cut the net free.

As we see-sawed our way through the rough sea we caught sight of three other row-boats two or three miles away. Their progress was so slow that it was difficult to know whether they were coming towards us or going in the opposite direction. I was assured, however, that they were the boats carrying the Cliffony, Magherow and Drumcliff police to Inismurray on the same mission as ourselves. It soon became evident that the boats were all making for the island and that the timing was 'according to schedule', as, judging by the distance that the boats were from the island, I realised that they should reach it at about the same time that we would.

There were then twelve families on Inismurray Island and when I saw the whole population, men, women and children, assembled on the shore I thought we were in for a hot reception. In this I was greatly mistaken, as, apart from the fact that there were no flags or bands, we could not have received a warmer welcome. The men actually came down to the water's edge to help us ashore and the women were not far behind in their display of genuine friendship. They knew all the policemen except myself and the police called them by their Christian names. A number of parcels which had been brought from the mainland were then distributed.

On practically every journey that the R.I.C. made to the island parcels of groceries and other messages, including letters, were brought out to the islanders. I later learned from the islanders that these parcels often contained supplies of treacle, yeast and barm for the manufacture of poteen and that some of the letters would contain orders for poteen from their customers on the mainland. They also informed me that they always knew when the police were due to call and that the illicit stills and poteen would be put on board one or more of their boats and rowed out west of the island where the oarsmen would devote their time to fishing until the R.I.C. left the island.

After about half an hour's conversation with the islanders we got down to business and set off in pairs to search for illicit stills and poteen.

Inismurray, which is twice as long as it is wide, is roughly two hundred statute acres with some reasonably good tillage and grazing land. Most of it, however, is barren and infertile. It has neither trees, rivers nor lakes and is completely exposed to the Atlantic gales. There are no proper landing places for boats, except for a few narrow creeks, so that in stormy weather boats cannot enter or leave the island. It is surrounded on all sides by huge boulders of rock, many tons in weight, and piled up in great profusion.

The island is deeply indented and in places there are caves at least twenty feet in height and penetrating in some cases to a depth which it is difficult to ascertain. The floors of the caves are strewn with rocks and up through these rocks the sea lashes its way throwing up great sheets of water and making a noise which is deafening. Indeed, we might as well have taken lead pencils instead of steel rods to probe for poteen in this difficult terrain, frequented only by hawks, swallows and martins. Never until that day in Inismurray did I realise that police-duty could be reduced to such a farce. Not only was it possible to conceal illicit stills and spirits but even a regiment of soldiers could be hidden in the rocks and caves of this remote island. Needless to say we made no captures that day. Having failed to destroy the sole industry of these friendly people we returned to the home of Mrs Harte who always provided tea for the police and revenue officers. The tea was excellent and the charge modest even for those days. And, believe it or not, at the end of our meal we were treated to a few glasses of poteen.

While we were having our tea a storm arose with thunder, lightning and torrential rain. As the day advanced the storm continued, and the question of our having to remain on the island was discussed. The islanders encouraged us to stay and made preparations for our doing so. The boatmen, when consulted on the advisability of returning to the mainland, shook their heads. Later in the day, however, the storm abated somewhat and we decided against the wishes of the boatmen to return

What I considered was a rough sea on the outward journey was, by comparison with the return journey, quite calm. Instead of high waves and deep ravines, the sea was now a mass of angry water and foam. Before we were half a mile from the island wave after wave swept over our little boat, at times half filling it with water, and keeping two men constantly bailing it out. I made no secret of the fact that I was terribly scared and one of the boatmen took advantage of this to produce a bottle of poteen which was passed around and all had a drink. Between the buffetting of the waves and the strong poteen I did not care whether the boat went up or down. I was unable even to help with the bailing out of the water. It was well after dark when we reached the mainland, exactly two miles from where we had intended landing. Even the sea-hardened boatmen were immensely relieved at getting ashore and said

that it was the worst crossing they had ever experienced. It was the first of many trips which I made to Inismurray on revenue duty.'

Constable Mee and his colleagues by then were at least able to get on to the island, even if they didn't seize too much — in contrast to the proud officers in the photo — but thirty five years or so previously it is doubtful if they would have set foot on the island, at least according to Inspector H.A. Robinson. Robinson was not a policeman and had been asked by the Government in 1881 to prepare a report on 'The state of the potato on the coast of Counties Galway and Sligo'. Accordingly he visited the area and his report contains some interesting information about the prevailing attitudes of the local people.

'I proceeded aboard HMS Bruiser (sic) on the 1st inst and visited the islands of Gonimna, Lettermore, Lettermullen, Dinish, Finish, Sherk, Crappagh,

Police seizure on Inishmurray Island. Constable Mee used to accompany men like these. (Public Record Office of N. Ireland)

Eragh, Inisnee, Omey, Boffin, Shark, Achil, Achilbeg and Iniskea, North and South ... the arrival of the Bruiser in Kilkieran Bay was the signal for the concentration of the united force of both sexes from all the surrounding islands to the landing place, duly prepared to accord an unenviable reception to what was at first regarded as a visit of a hostile nature. They expected to be processed for rent, which was the reason they subsequently assigned for the demonstration, but it is also probable that the guilty consciences of the proprietors of the illicit whiskey stills felt troubled as HM gunboat was seen threading her way through the narrow passes of the rocky bay. The police have recently made repeated raids on these stills and they believe that the illicit whiskey is manufactured to a considerable extent on the islands and sold in large quantities throughout the country.'

Robinson goes on to say that since the land is so poor and the kelp (seaweed) trade has declined so much he could readily see that the local people had no other means of making a living and he gives us a brief account of landing the next day on Iniskea. 'As in Kilkieran the arrival of the gunboat here was regarded as the forerunner of some unfriendly action and before I was permitted to land information as to the object and nature of my visit was sought.
''Were the polis on board?''
''No.''
''Where was I from then?''
''From the Local Government Board.''
A hurried consultation then followed and, as no evidence was forthcoming of the LGB having ever betrayed any animosity towards the poitin I was suffered to land at once.'

The RIC undercover poteen squad.
(T. W. Battle)

RIC Code 1888, amended 1911, Section 1667. The person in command of seizing party is to satisfy himself as to the genuineness of the wash, pot ale etc, seized and destroyed at the time of the seizure, by testing the liquid and obliging every man of the party to do the same. (Colman Doyle)

'The game's a good 'un.' (Colman Doyle)

The years 1918-22 saw an upsurge in the production of poitin. Whiskey was in short supply so demand for poitin increased with the R.I.C. occupied fighting the IRA. However, in some areas while the poitin maker may have thought he had a free hand from the attentions of the R.I.C. he did have to contend with the local Republican courts, for many of the Volunteers opposed the sale of poitin just as strongly as the English. And so in the West of Ireland, where the Sinn Fein policed the villages themselves some poitin makers found themselves parading in front of the congregation after Sunday Mass, heavily fined and forced to break up their own stills.

There is an account of this in 'Tales from the R.I.C.' published in 1921. It is a blatantly pro-British and anti-Irish book, full of slanders against the Sinn Feiners and praising the 'restraint' exercised by the gallant Black and Tans but it does paint a picture of the local Sergeant himself involved in the distribution of poitin by night while nominally seeking it by day. The author — anoymous but believed to be A.W. Long — describes how a Welshman, David Evans, rented an old mansion in Connaught which its owner didn't occupy while the war for Independence was going on, and set up a big still in the attic. He imported treacle in bulk, forsaking the old barley recipes, and arranged a network of distribution ranging from 'tea carts' (carts used by grocers to visit outlying areas) and creamery vans to the mail carts. Evans, it is claimed, escaped the wrath of the Sinn Fein and the R.I.C. and retired, a wealthy man when Independence came.

Extracts from the RIC Code (1888, amended 1911) concerning poitin   *1654. Warrant*

Although by the 18th section of Act 1 and 2 Wm IV excise officers are fully empowered to enter by DAY or by NIGHT all suspected houses and places WITHOUT warrant — to search for any private or concealed still or vessels used in illicit distillation — or any spirit, low wines, &c; preparing or prepared for distillation, or for any illegally made malt, corn, or grain — this power should not be exercised unless the suspicion or information be such as will fully justify the act — for it is to be remembered that by the latter part of the same section, it is the actual FINDING of any of the articles referred to therein that will be a full justification in the event of their proceedings being called to question. The more prudent and advisable course in all doubtful cases will therefore be to obtain a magistrate's warrant, as directed by the 17th section of the Act in question.

1658. Equipment for Revenue Duty.

A party on revenue duty is not to consist of less than three men. At stations where revolvers are available, they will be carried instead of carbines, but otherwise carbines should be carried. One of the party, who will have charge of the imperial gallon measure, should not, in any circumstances, carry a carbine. He will carry two pairs of handcuffs, one on each side of waist belt, for which purpose an extra handcuff-case may be issued to stations where this duty is performed. Sword bayonets need not be carried by any of the men.

1667. Testing seizure

The person in command of seizing party is to satisfy himself as to the genuineness of the wash, potale, etc, seized and destroyed at the time of seizure, by tasting the liquid, and obliging every man of the party to do the same.

1668. Destruction of Seizure

All malt or grain liable to seizure is to be destroyed by burning it, but if on the sea coast, it may be thrown into the sea. All illicit malt houses and still houses are to be completely destroyed.

Irish Republican Courts were in existence from 1918 to 1922. They were predominantly a rural phenomenon but did exist in some of the larger towns as well. This was during the war of Independence when the policy of boycotting all English institutions was at its height and many people preferred to turn to the local IRA or Sinn Fein to settle their differences with their neighbours rather than rely on the R.I.C. or the landed gentry magistrates. Sinn Fein obviously encouraged this and accordingly Republican Courts, which met of course in secret, were set up.

Many today look back and cite these courts as in some way a revolutionary development but in fact they rarely were. Often the judges in these courts while full of nationalistic fervour were also extremely conservative. For example, they usually ruled in favour of the large landlord when the peasants tried to take over landed estates and found co-operatives or Soviets. In the light of such reactionary attitudes it becomes easier to understand why they were so opposed to the local poitin maker, who was forced to parade in front of the congregation before Mass and witness the smashing of his still. Most members of Sinn Fein in those days were Pioneers, total abstainers, and to many of them the poitin maker represented a corrupting influence in the area. Moreover, if the 'boys' were always drinking poitin they would be less likely to be out training and drilling. This was somewhat ironic since many poitin makers were enthusiastic Republicans whose knowledge of the hills and countryside had often helped the 'boys' on the run. In some areas, for instance Munterloney in the Sperrins, this lost Republicans a lot of support.

The puritan streak in Sinn Fein and the IRA continued for quite a few years however. For example, in Belfast in the 1940s it was almost impossible to find an IRA man who smoked or drank.

Such things were frowned on. Times have changed a lot in that respect, but, between 1918 and 1922 many Sinn Feiners felt that they had to exercise their 'authority' by 'keeping law and order' — and shooting R.I.C. men and Black and Tans.

THE JUDGES DISAGREE

'People who manufacture and sell poteen are as bad as if not worse than those who sell drugs.'
Mr Justice Kenny. 6/11/73.

'I hear it's a great rub for the lumbago.'
Mr Justice O'Farrell. 14/1/77.

After fining a man £6 instead of £200 or jailing him:
'It seems this outdated Act leaves me no option, but if I had my way I'd take certain steps in relation to cases like this. It seems ridiculous that after fifty of self government we can do nothing about this.'
Mr Justice Shaw. 15/3/72.

Garda pose before smashing still. Note unhappy gardai second left. (Irish Times)

Patrol 6. 9. 92, This patrol made a careful and exhausted search in the mountains of Dully and Teprone for illicit shifts or trace of same but we got nothing the appears to be nothing of the sort going on in that pa of Sub. District I had som talk with people throug the Country they appear to be very content & happy, were it not for the bad price of Ca & Sheep the mountains is completely covered with th

Matt. Lynam

CHAPTER 3   IN THE MOST UNUSUAL PLACES

By the very nature of its illegality, poitin has always been made in secret. In the past, even in the fastness of the Donegal mountains where no revenue man set foot from year to year, the still was always hidden and a round the clock watch kept, usually by children, in case prying eyes discovered the secret location. Elaborate booby traps were often laid, hidden ditches or pits where the unwary might tumble and break a leg. Caves, carefully camouflaged, were frequently used and of course for many, islands were ideal. Sometimes secret rooms were built into houses where the distiller could work unseen — the main problem being how to get rid of the telltale smoke and smell. (In one case I've heard of the distillers opted for brazen cheek. They inhabited a house which was attached to the local police station and shared a common chimney. They lasted several years without being detected although the still was under the police's noses and when finally caught were let off, since to bring the case to court would have been too embarrassing for the police.) Carleton describes a deep cave, running 'under the rocks which met over it in a kind of Gothic arch: a stream of water fell in through a fissure from above forming a subterranean cascade in the cavern.' Here the poitin maker worked.

In his book 'Lovely is the Lee' Gibbings relates how, not far from Macroom in County Cork he was walking over the mountains when 'coming suddenly over the crest of a hillock, I thought, for a moment, that I saw two small men disappear into the ground before me; indeed, I was positive that I'd seen them, yet there was no sign. Stories of fairy mounds and raths flashed into my mind. ''What the hell are you doing here?'' asked a man at my shoulder. ''Trying to find my way back to Gougane Barra'' I replied.' (After explaining who he is and being recognised as having been vouched for, Gibbings is taken into the secret place.)

'From three sides of the landscape there wasn't the slightest suggestion of a cave, but, on the fourth side, from which we now entered, it was surprisingly open. The roof was one huge slab of flat stone, heavily overgrown with moss and tufts of heather. It was supported in front by two large boulders, its back being deeply embedded in the rock. Any gaps at the sides had been filled in with sods of turf and heather. It was as natural a hiding place as one could imagine. Inside, a fire had just been lit under a large three-legged pot that rested on two low walls of stone. I noticed that the wooden lid of the pot had been sealed along its edge, as if with putty; soap and linseed meal, I was later told. From a kind of hood on the lid a tapered copper pipe led to an angular coil. ''They're better angular, the angles throw the steam from side to side.'' This coil disappeared into a barrel of water, but its nose protruded through a hole near the bottom. Under the nose a stoneware gallon jar stood, as if expectant. Flanking the barrel of water there were two other barrels covered with sacks and flat stones. One at least, contained sprouting barley.'

Gibbings was then subjected to the traditional hospitality of the West Cork distiller, which, I can confirm is often overwhelming. It was near the spot described above that I was brought down a pot hole in a fairy rath in the dead of night to be shown a secret chamber, used, it was alleged, in the past by local poitin makers. After this somewhat uncomfortable trip we had to stay up half the night trying to distinguish the difference between 'Mid Cork No.1' and 'Mid Cork No.2' poitin.

Nowadays, with illicit distillation going on in many towns, a whole new set of sites are being used. As reported earlier by Caesar Otway, in Erris a chapel was often used in the past and while this may not go on at present, in our large cities school labs, hospital labs and back garden sheds and garages are being used for making their own version of 'the cratur'. The present troubles have meant increased army and police presence on the roads and as a result the poitin maker is now more wary about transporting his finished product too far. In parts of South Derry or Tyrone for example you'd do yourself no good at all to be seen acting furtively with a beer keg or milk churn. As a result, in the North of Ireland at least, many urban poitin drinkers, denied their regular supply from the country have taken to setting up

Above Left:
Small boys guard still, c 1880. (*Welch Collection, Ulster Museum*)

*The police above were raiding premises at 9
Milford Place in the Pound Loney, Belfast,
3rd April, 1921, for guns and got a real
shock instead—they stumbled on the first
illicit still ever to be captured on the Falls.*

Right:
Poitin mural, 1945. All the characters are
recognizable locals. The man inside the hill
with folded arms is in fact the local RIC
Inspector. (*The Falls Hotel, Ennistymon,
Co Clare*)

secret stills in the city. It's less romantic than 'up on the moss' but more comfortable.

The most bizarre setting for a still that I've come across is actually inside a hollowed out giant redwood tree in California, but, alas, the Revenue men have confiscated the still and padlocked up the tree. What a dreadful waste of human ingenuity! Another place where ingenuity is needed to make poitin is in our jails, and yet, for over a century at least, the craft has gone on, behind bars, using an amazing range of improvised equipment. The next section is taken from interviews with ex-internees who, while inside, didn't let their distilling talents go to waste.

Prison Poitin

In Crumlin Road jail in the 1940s they were unable to make poitin, but, undeterred, they proceeded to make a vile concoction from prune juice. One veteran who survived this, nearly forty years afterwards still recalled the foul taste and the hilarity whenever the jars containing the fermenting juice started to explode under the prisoners' beds. Those incarcerated in Derry Jail were luckier and, thanks to the skills of P.S. (still alive) were able to sample a superior product which had been made on an improvised still. The main problem that arose at that time was not one of getting the potatoes or using the cookhouse boiler, but of circumventing the church, for the chief distiller's accomplice, P.M. was a devout Catholic and insisted on mentioning the distilling when he made his confession. To his horror he was told that poitin making was a reserved sin in the diocese and that he would have to confess to the bishop, an impossible task in his present situation.

In the Republic of Ireland prisons poitin was made too. Sean Lyons who was a sentenced prisoner in Mountjoy jail recalls how he and 'Cushie' Ryan experimented with dandelion wine, picking the dandelions in the prison yard and getting yeast smuggled in by a friendly screw. Cushie, using stolen food tins, stolen matches and the pages from the cell's Bible, boiled up a concoction which, although not great, was very welcome at Christmas along with the smuggled whiskey. That was in 1940 and Lyons had to wait four more years before he could try his hand at something more potent.

In 1943 he was transferred with other Republican prisoners to the Curragh Internment camp. There he met Ned Gallagher, a Mayo man and a veteran distiller. With Ashe Hughes, Tommy Griffen, Roger Ryan, Liam Cotter and Tom Kiely they formed 'the poitin gang', determined to make Christmas '43 a day to remember. It was. Yeast was smuggled in to a sick prisoner who claimed that 'it was the only thing that would settle his stomach.' Porridge meal was secreted away regularly by the cooks. A length of galvanised piping was ripped off a disused hut and used for a worm and ¼ inch diameter rubber tubing was stolen from a car. Sean Lyons, a cabinet maker by trade, ingeniously fashioned a circular lid from a plank taken from one of the prisoner's beds and Ned Gallagher announced that he wasn't going to Mass any more. This was because when all the other prisoners and officers were attending Mass he could use the cookhouse boiler.

All was nearly ready. Helpers were dispatched to scour the jail for bottles, and many's the 'sick' man applied to the doctor for a cough bottle. According to Lyons, the laziest person in the jail at the time was Brendan Behan. He was too lazy to get out of bed to relieve himself and used to have a secret store of empty bottles under his bed, which, after they had been filled, he used to hurl out of the window. These were discovered by an unsuspecting 'beachcomber' who had been told to go and scavenge for empty bottles. The bottles were all rinsed out and used, but as Sean Lyons said, 'those in the know made damn sure we knew which bottles were which.' Brendan was duly presented at Christmas with one of his old bottles containing Curragh poitin.

The cookhouse now became the focus of attention. An old unused boiler was commandeered, a lid fashioned for it, and shirts draped around it ostensibly to dry but really to act as a camouflage. Oatmeal was put in one of the kitchen's milkchurns and put aside to ferment. This was a bit dangerous as the fermenting meal made loud noises from time to time but fortunately the screw was old and almost deaf. Finally, 'D' day arrived and Gallagher retired alone to the cookhouse while everyone else went to Mass. The contents of the churn were poured into the boiler, the rim was sealed with dough, and the lid weighted down with stones. Then the boiler was

lit. Lyons described the magic moment when, returning from Mass, they crept in to the cookhouse. ' "How's it going Ned?"
"Not too well."
And then "blurb, blurb," and there it was, the first drop falling into the bucket.' Within an hour they had a bucketful bottled and another hour later the still was dismantled and hidden away. 'I'll always remember that Christmas day and the shouting and singing and celebrating' says Sean.

In the 1940s poitin was only made in jails for very special occasions and this is still true today. However, in Long Kesh, they tend to have quite a few 'special days' and most cages have their own stills. 'Uncle Doc', who did several years as an internee in Long Kesh tells how he used to make stills with the available equipment.

Long Kesh 1977. Note Burco boiler. In Long Kesh poitin was known as 'special powers.'

'It was quite easy really. The cage system meant that at night you would all be locked up in the one hut, and the screws wouldn't come round until next morning. I would strip a ½ inch diameter copper pipe from the toilet, fill it with dry salt, plug the ends, warm it and bend it. (The salt is to stop the pipe crimping). That would make a reasonable worm. I'd use potatoes or brown sugar or fruit and make the wash using empty food trays which had a good lid. Yeast was no problem to smuggle in. Then the wash would be put into the Burco boiler. Every hut had one of these. I'd use back up nuts and brown paper washers to tighten the connections and run the hose to the water tap. Weights on top of the lid, a regular supply of water to regulate the temperature, bread and water paste to block any leaks and off you'd go. The first run would come out and be caught in half of a large plastic fruit juice container. We normally always drank the singlings rather than give it a second run. This meant that although we got drunk we generally got shocking hangovers because the fusel oil hadn't been eliminated, but, what the hell, you needed something to cheer you up. Working steadily I'd get 2½-3 gallons three times a day. Since by no means all the men in the hut would be drinkers this was more than enough for a good party to celebrate escapes, birthdays, anniversaries or Christmas. Most cages had their own stills. The screws knew it was going on of course, I'm not giving away any big secrets, but it didn't worry them. Why should it?'

From talking to other ex-prisoners you learn that nowadays nearly every jail in the country has its illicit distillers, including the women's jails in Armagh and Limerick and the more you talk to them the more you become convinced that some people, even if tied in a strait jacket, chained to the wall and kept in solitary confinement in a dungeon cell would still be able to work out some way to make 'the stuff'. As R.W. Grimshaw said, 'the only limits to the use of alcohol is your imagination.'

EVEN THE DANES ARE AT IT

The following is a simple Danish recipe. The end product is remarkably like poitin.

''Fill a 25 litre plastic container with water. Add 6 kilos of sugar and about 350 grammes of brewer's yeast, together with a small quantity of margerine. (The margerine is to cut down the number of yeast bubbles.) Seal tightly and leave to ferment for 3—4 weeks, until the yeast is exhausted. When no further sound can be heard, you are ready to distill. The process can be speeded by adding a small amount of ammonium carbinate is desired.

The mixture is then decanted into a very large distillation flask or a steel container. For efficient separation a fractionating column is necessary and this is best made oneself. Get a stainless steel tube, about 5cm in diameter and 120cm in length. Fill with small pieces of glass tubing of about ½cm diameter and about 1—2 cm long. If you can't get small glass tubes, ceramic ones will do. Then cork the column into the distillation flask. At the top of the column add a water cooled condenser, and a centigrade thermometer.

Next, heat the flask slowly, watching the temperature. Some liquid will condense at lower than 76°C. Discard this. Collect only that liquid which condenses between 76°C and 80°C. (78°C is the boiling of alcohol.)

Mix 50-50 with water and for every 2 litres, add 5 grams of Potassium Permanganate. This will give you an undrinkable purple solution. Filter this, preferably through activated charcoal, and leave for two days.

Then set up your equipment again and distill as before. When the temperature reaches 78°C there

The barrels contain fish—and at times poitin smuggled from the island to the mainland. (Lawrence Collection, National Library of Ireland)

should be no yeasty smell and you will be collecting pure alcohol. It is important not to distill too quickly. About 2 drops per second is quite fast enough. Again, as soon as the temperature rises over 80°C, stop the process. This will give you 96% pure alcohol and you must dilute this to about 40% by adding distilled water. In Scandanavia (and in Ireland) you can buy a wide variety of essences to produce whatever flavour you want.

Extra hints: Since sugar and yeast take some time to mix properly, it is best to grind up ½ kilo of sugar with the yeast while dissolving the rest of the sugar in the water. Then add the sugar/yeast mixture, top up to 25 litres and add just a teaspoonfull of margerine.

Use large corks or rubber bungs for the joints between the flask and the fractionating column and the column and the condenser. The glass tubing between the latter two should be at least 1½ cm in diameter.

The alcoholic concentration of water/alcohol mixtures can be gauged from hydrometer measurements of the specific gravity.

For an even purer product, distill for the third time, although this is not absolutely necessary.

MEANWHILE, IN THE AFRICAN DESERT

Michael John O'Reilly, a Tipperary man teaching at the University of Tripoli in Libya was, in March 1977 tried and convicted in a Libyan court for distilling alcohol, which is, of course, strictly forbidden under Koranic law. He was sentenced to two years imprisonment but appealed, claiming that since it was coming up to St Patricks Day he had merely being following local Irish customs and making a holy drink in honour of the Saint to be drunk by Libya's substantial expatriate community. The Court solemnly debated this impassioned plea and reduced his sentence to a suspended one, setting him free. He didn't get his poitin back however!

In Arab countries quite a lot of illicit distillation goes on, and not only by the Irish. When the author was working in Saudi Arabia in 1966 a form of second rate poitin known as 'Sediki', which is Arabic for 'my friend' was made on a commercial basis by several Americans. It sold for £1 a bottle and was fairly vile. In Libya today the stuff is called 'Flash', presumably for its cleansing properties and it retails at £10 a litre, though the better stuff can be halved with water. It is a big business. Home distilleries change hands for large sums when the owner leaves for healthier climes. In May 1977 an Englishman trying to emulate O'Reilly was busted by the Libyan police who found six stills and £26,000 Libyan Dinars (£52,000). But then, the English never could sucessfully make Whiskey!

I am indebted to Mr Edmund Mahoney of the Bounder of Adventure Travel Agency for this story.

7TH CENTURY RECIPE FOR USQUEBAGH

'Mace, cloves, cinnamon, ginger, coriander, cubebs, raisins, liquorice, sugar and saffron. Well dissevered and put into a linen cloth and hung at the worm's end, whereby all the tincture will be extracted and run amonst the distilled goods.'

(This obviously can't be a genuine Irish recipe since most of the ingredients were never seen in Ireland, but it does appear to date to the 7th century. Origin seems Eastern which seems reasonable since the first distillers were almost certainly Arabs and Egyptians. The first alembics [or old stills] were made in Egypt. The word 'Alcohol' comes from the Arabic 'al-kohl'. While Arabs were forbidden by the Koran to drink alcohol, their Christian enemies had no such scruples. *From The Red Book of Ossory*

CHAPTER 4 POITIN GOES TO AMERICA

Poitin was brought to America primarily by the Scots-Irish Ulsterman. The first big wave of emigration from Ulster to the 'new colonies' came in the years 1717-1720. Six years of drought had ruined the flax and decimated the linen industry, sheep rot had struck in 1716, there was a smallpox epidemic in 1718 and on top of all that rack renting landlords were becoming even more rapacious than usual. It seemed a good time to move. America offered the opportunity to 'be your own man', to get away from the dominance of the monarchy and the church of England. Most would go as indentured servants, only a few could afford the passage on their own, but go they did and by 1776 it is estimated that some 350,000 Ulstermen and women were established in the Eastern seaboard counties of America. With them they had brought their religion, generally Presbyterianism, their thriftiness, their industry and their talent for making 'John Barleycorn'.

In early days in the colonies, it is claimed, the local water was suspect — this at least is the reason given for the proliferation of alcoholic beverages made from apples, pears, pumpkins, parsnips, walnuts, plums, whortleberries, turnips, carrots, persimmons — in fact from virtually every fruit or vegetable available. The still house, a windowless log cabin was often the centre of village life and the new Ulster colonist, with his experience of poitin making was in great demand.

The name 'Moonshine', which soon came to be applied to all illicit corn liquor derives from 'moonlighter' and was originally used in England to describe the brandy smugglers who landed at night bringing their contraband from Holland and the low countries to thirsty English customers. In some parts of the States, notably North Carolina, Southwest Virginia and Georgia itself illicit distillers were often called 'blockaders', but throughout we'll stick to the more common term 'moonshiner'. (Bootlegging of course is only really concerned with selling illegal whiskey and not producing it, although occasionally the two functions were combined).

At first, as in Ireland, distilling was perfectly legal. Whiskey was not taxed in America until 1791 and throughout the 18th century the pioneers continued to drink large amounts of every conceivable kind of spirit not only for the intoxicating effect but also because alcohol of all kinds was regarded as of medicinal use for young and old alike. At this time the most popular drink was 'bumbo' — a mixture of rum, sugar, water and nutmeg and many's the famous person who swore by it. George Washington for example was, he admitted, only finally elected after two failures because he purchased for the 391 electors 169 gallons of rum, wine, beer and cider. His election expenses amounted to £39.7s — of which £34 was for drink.

The Ulster-Irish poured in. Indians, like the Shawnees who had the temerity to get in their way were ruthlessly attacked. Down the great valley between the Appalachian and Blue Ridge mountains they poured for almost forty years. They were

acquisitive, belligerent and were to form the backbone of the resistance to English rule when the revolution broke out. They were also canny. It made good economic sense to convert your grain into whiskey. H.F. Wilkie explains the economics of it thus: 'the yield from rye distillation was a gallon of whiskey for each 1½ bushels of grain. One pack horse could carry two eight gallon kegs of whiskey, or the equivalent of 24 bushels of grain. In its solid form corn or barley would only bring 25 cents a bushel; a horse therefore could only carry two dollars worth, but with a whiskey cargo the horse's payload rose to at least 16 dollars, the asking price for whiskey being at least a dollar a gallon.' So it wasn't just an inherited taste for 'the hard stuff'. Corn whiskey was the common man's best cash crop. A good still was a very necessary appendage to any farm. And so the pioneers continued their rugged and dangerous existence, fighting the Indians, the environment and the would be landlords who laid claim to the virgin territory. They fought with Washington and Morgan and Nelson and 'Nolichucky Jack' Sevier and repulsed the British under Cornwallis and Ferguson, and while they fought for American Indpendence their daily ration included half a pint of whiskey. After Independence they expected to get their just reward and be left in peace. It was not to be.

A member of the North Georgia Moonshine Klan, the Honest Man's Friend and Protector. (Joseph E. Dabney)

Right:
'The family that distils together, stays together.' Kentucky moonshiners, c 1930.

On March 3rd 1791 Congress, greedy as all Governments are, voted in favour of Alexander Hamilton's scheme. In order to pay off the country's 21 million dollar war debt henceforth whiskey production would be taxed. Praising Hamilton's scheme Daniel Webster was to say 'he smote the rock of the national resources and abundant streams of revenue gushed forth.' The average pioneer didn't see it that way. To him it was rank treachery. A savage attack on his livelihood and his independence. Down the Monongaheala River the word spread. 'Pay no excise on whiskey'. Bands of vigilantes, often going under the mythical leadership of 'Tom the Tinker' went round assaulting any excise men brave — or foolhardy — enough to demand the tax. Those who did pay often had their stills wrecked by their neighbours who resented such spinelessness. For three years revolt simmered and little if any whiskey tax was collected in the frontier areas around the Monongaheala. Then the Government tried to assert itself. In July 1794 the U.S. District court at Philadelphia issued warrants against 75 known distillers who were refusing to pay the iniquitous tax. The subsequent refusal to pay this was to lead to the Whiskey Rebellion.

Of course it was not all about a tax on whiskey. Many people had vested interests in asserting 'States Rights' against the federal authorities. Then too, rumours were rife. It was alleged, and widely believed, that Congress was extending the excise levy to ploughs at a dollar a time, that every wagon entering Philadelphia would have to pay a toll of one dollar, that Pittsburgh was going to introduce a birth tax of 15 shillings for the birth of every boy and ten shillings for the birth of every girl. Such stories were in fact totally untrue, but to the suspicious, independent minded and truculent pioneer they were but more proof of the Federal authorities' perfidy. Washington tried to calm the situation down by sending commissioners to Pittsburgh who would grant amnesties for any past offences to those who signed an oath of allegiance and promised in the future to pay the hated excise but this only incited the would-be insurgents all the more. 'Damn cheek' was the consensus of opinion, and who, in all conscience could dispute that. And so the 'rebellion' broke out.

The Whiskey Rebellion

In fact, the rebellion of 1794 was pretty ignominious for the distillers. After a couple of marches to Pittsburgh by the rebels — who were royally received by the local residents who feared that they might fire the town — Philadelphia determined on action. Washington ordered the troops out, nearly 13,000 of them drawn from Virginia, Maryland and Pennsylvania, and marched them in two groups down the Monongaheala. The whiskey rebels, who had at one time numbered over two thousand faded away. The federal troops made a few arrests, meted out some summary and vicious punishment and returned triumphant to Philadelphia on Christmas day with 17 'Insurgents'. An anti-climax, but none the less it had shown that the new Federal government intended to assert its authority. They had in fact spent 1½ million dollars to put this revolt down and used more men than they had for much of the war of Independence. Thus they had spent more than an entire year's whiskey tax would bring in. Moreover, 15 of the 17 scapegoats were acquitted and the two 'guilty' men pardoned. Hamilton felt that it had all been worthwhile however. Those Westerners had been shown who ruled.

The disgruntled distillers moved Southwest, pushing back the Indians and establishing Kentucky and Tennessee while consolidating Georgia and the Carolinas. In these states the great common denominator was corn; it could be eaten, drunk or slept upon and was the staple crop for most. And each time a new settlement opened up, one of the first structures built was the stillhouse. Revenge was at hand too, for in 1800 the Hamiltonian Federalists were defeated at the polls. In came Democrat Jefferson, one of whose first actions was to end 'that damned whiskey tax'. The West rejoiced. No more excise, no more gaugers or Revenue men. And so it was to continue until 1862, with the brief exception of the war of 1812, the golden age of excise-free distillation. By 1819 Tennessee was turning out an estimated 800,000 gallons of whiskey a year. New Orleans, one of the main distribution centres for the trade was handling 2 million gallons a year from up river. Bourbon had been invented and was becoming popular. Drink was cheap — 25 cents a gallon — and there were no revenue men or temperance societies to bother the drinking man.

It couldn't last of course. Sixty years was a good run, but sooner or later the Government had to interfere again. In 1862, needing money to continue the Civil War, Congress re-imposed the excise on John Barleycorn. In 1863 it was assessed at 20 cents a gallon. Within two years it had risen to 2 dollars. (Today it is 10.50 dollars). Immediately the civil war ended the carpet baggers descended upon the South. In their wake came the revenue men. They had their work cut out. Some distillers it is true made a show of complying with the law. They registered and became owners of 'government stills'; but corruption, trickery and good old fashioned bribery meant that the amount they were supposed to be producing by day was frequently substantially augmented by the amount produced at night.

Most Appalachian mountain men scorned such subterfuges. The Commissioner of Internal Revenue reported in 1877:

'I can safely say that during the past year not less than 3,000 illicit stills have been operated in this area of the Appalachians. These stills are producing 10 to 50 gallons a day. They are usually located at inaccessible points in the mountains ... and are generally owned by unlettered men of desperate character ... armed and ready to resist the officers of the law. Where occasion requires, they come together in companies of from ten to fifty persons, gun in hand, to drive the officers out of the county.'

Ten dollars was the standard fee for informers but there were few takers. On top of an inbred hatred of touts and informers many mountain men had a healthy desire to stay alive. They knew only too well that touts had a habit of mysteriously disappearing. In Pickens County, Georgia, in 1889 twenty seven local moonshiners even formed their own Moonshiners Klu Klux Klan, called 'The honest man's friend and protector'. Seven of them were subsequently convicted of arson, the burning of suspected touts' homes.

So the Revenue men had to do it themselves. Disguised as peddlers or trappers they would descend on an area and try to sniff out the moonshiners and their stills. One trick was to try to find a stream where one's horse wouldn't drink. This was regarded as a sure sign that still slops had been thrown in upstream. Alternatively the revenue man could pretend to be a hunter or fisherman, but local people were rarely fooled. J. B. Crutcher quotes from the memoirs of Joe Spurrier, a Revenue man who was sent to the East Tennessee mountains in the 1880s.

'The moonshiners found out I was in the mountains before I fully knew the fact myself. And the way they spread the information would do credit to a long distance telephone. The first man that heard of me blew a horn. I think he had a certain number of toots for my name. The horn could be heard three miles, and everyone within hearing took

A 520 gallon 'Silver Cloud' pot still captured in Cooke County, Tennessee. Note the two flues going through the galvanised still pot. This still was fired by liquified petroleum gas. The photograph suggests why so-called 'silver clouds', very popular in the Cosky (Cooke County) area of East Tennessee, are said to resemble a 'silver cloud' on a hill side, particularly at night under the light of a bright moon. (Joseph E. Dabney)

Right:

A steamer still being destroyed in North Georgia during the 1940s. Officer in front is cutting hoops and smashing apart huge mash barrels, with the white, foamy, fermenting mash pouring out. The upright boiler at left is surrounded by a brick wall to help conserve the heat. (Joseph E. Dabney 'Mountain Spirits')

up the alarm till the echoes were awakened by the sound of the horns. In an hour after the first blast people one hundred miles away knew that Spurrier was on a raid. I didn't get a dog's chance to seize a distillery.' (The same warning system was used in Ireland at times).

The Revenue men had some successes of course. They claimed that between 1877 and 1881 they captured almost 5,000 stills and made 8,000 arrests while losing 29 agents with a further 63 being seriously injured. Famous Revenue men like Captain James Davis became the bane of the moonshiner's life. He was frequently involved in shoot-outs and seiges and claimed the credit for capturing such infamous moonshiners as Campbell Morgan, 'the monarch of the Tennessee moonshiners' and old man Bill Berong, both of whom, to their shame, upon capture turned revenue men themselves to save their skin. Davis himself was finally shot in an ambush by an anonymous moonshiner in the Tennessee mountains.

The war against the moonshiner continued unabated, and the mountainy men fought back. It is often said that the introduction of prohibition in 1920 was a shot in the arm to the illicit distilling trade and this is obviously true for some areas, but in the moonshine country liquor in fact had been banned for years. Georgia voted out whiskey in 1907 and Alabama, Mississippi, North Carolina and Tennessee soon followed. By 1917 Virginia and West Virginia were also 'dry'. In all, when the US entered the war 26 states were officially dry. This was of course completely hypocritical. In these states one could not legally buy liquor or sell it in a saloon but, if licensed, you could manufacture it since the revenue accruing from this 'evil' was very useful for both State and Federal authorities. And so the Southern States continued to 'vote dry and drink wet' even up to the 1960s. (Will Rodgers, with hand on heart, assured a journalist that his state would remain dry as 'long as the citizens can stagger to the polls to vote'.)

Prohibition did make bootlegging big business of course and naturally organised crime, crooked politicians and policemen on the make took advantage of it. General Lincoln Andrews of the Prohibition Enforcement Bureau estimated in 1925 that half a million Americans were involved in moonshining and/or bootlegging. In that year alone his agents seized 172,537 stills but even the General admitted that that was only the tip of the iceberg. For every still captured, nine continued to operate. Much of the stuff made was vile tasting and in many cases highly dangerous. The unscrupulous were out for a quick buck and didn't care who they maimed or killed with their poisonous 'Smoke', 'Jake', 'Nigger Gin', 'Yack yack bourbon', 'Stingo', 'Soda Pop Moon' or 'Straightsville Stuff'. Henry Lee in 'How dry we were' reckons also that through deliberately poisoning such substances as Jamaica ginger and industrial alcohol, both used by moonshiners, with benzine, nicotine, mercury and aldehyde, the Government blinded, paralyzed or killed thousands of drinkers.' 'Jake', a poisonous concoction of almost 90% alcohol fluid extract Jamaica ginger with wood alcohol added, permanently paralyzed at least 15,000 people. Thousands more were killed through experimenting with idiot recipes.

In the South money grabbing was just as prevalent. Old moonshiners were appalled at the rapid changes that came over the trade. 'The pride of the calling has departed, moonshining, once a gentleman's avocation, is now a business' said one ruefully. The enormous profits to be made tempted all but the most fastidious and the invention of the 'thumper' keg helped to destroy old traditions. This eliminated the time consuming second run. The thumper, about 50 gallons in volume was put between the cooking pot and the condenser and filled with beer. Hot vapour sent bubbling up through the thumper beer produced a second distillation. From this men went on to develop the 'steamer' or 'stack steamer', two or three giant metal drums welded together. This meant up to three hundred gallons of moonshine could be made in the one giant pot in one day. Worse still, the old traditional ingredient, grain meal was disgarded. Steadily most of the meal was replaced with corn sugar, readily available cheaply from farmers in the Mid-West. Dabney quotes the following staggering profit margins:— 5 dollars would buy 100 pounds of sugar, which would produce ten gallons of high proof moonshine which would sell at anything from 20 to 40 dollars a gallon. If the hooch was then watered down a man could easily turn his 5 dollars into 500 dollars. At the height of the depression the traditional penalty of a year and a day in the 'Pen' was unlikely to deter too many people. In Atlanta half of the 2,200 prisoners were inside on moonshine offences. In the 1930s in Franklin County, a small area in the Appalachian foothills of Virginia, it was estimated that over a four year period 3½ million gallons were successfully made.

Prohibition ended in 1933, moonshining did not. Many of the Southern states, traditionally the moonshiner's heartland, retained the 'local option' which meant that, officially at least, they were dry. But the heart had gone out of the old moonshining. Commercial interests had taken over and quality suffered. Moonshining still goes on of course. In 1972, the latest figures I have been able to get, the U.S. Treasury department destroyed 2,090 illicit distilleries and poured down the sink some million and a quarter gallons of mash and 67,000 gallons of whiskey, and even they accept that they are only scratching the surface. It is their estimate that moonshiners in America produce some 9 million gallons of the stuff a year, defrauding, they moan, the Revenue men of 97 million dollars and state tax men of 35 million dollars. By Irish standards this seems a vast enterprise, but, compared with the thirties it is 'small beer'. The old time moonshiners lament the passing of an era and scorn the modern 'get rich quick' mentality of today's entrepeneur. Let us conclude this brief chapter with an account of what it was like in the old days to make moonshine in the Appalachians. It comes from Arthur Young, who was born in 1903 and lived and distilled in the Smoky mountains in North Carolina. This extract is from an interview he gave Joseph Dabney in 1972.

Up on Smoky Mountain

'First of all I always made sure that I had my equipment made by a skilled still maker. Next I'd select a good secluded spot in the mountains beside a clean, clear stream, get some rocks from the bed of the stream and build a small furnace. Then I got a copper tube, three quarters or an inch in diameter and about sixteen, eighteen feet long — long enough so that when it is curled, it would go from the bottom of a fifty-gallon barrel to the top. I'd pour either sand or sawdust in the tube to keep it from crimping and twist it around a stump. Then I'd place this worm inside the barrel and fit the top of the tube to the cap arm from the still. Never used a thump keg. Went directly from the pot to the worm. I'd put a trough into the barrel — a flake stand — and run cold water through it all the time.

If you had a fifty gallon still you'd need about eight bushels of meal-ground from choice white corn only. You'd start with eight 50 gallon barrels and put a half bushel of meal in each one. Then you cook-in the other half of the meal, four bushels, in your still pot. Just heat it up and make it mushy. Then you divide that back into the barrels so that each barrel

The war against moonshiners in Muskogee County, Oklahoma, in the 1920s netted this result — stills of all varieties. The campaign against the illicit whisky makers was led by Sherrif J. F. Ledbetter (fourth from left) who won the nickname of 'Stillbuster.' (Joseph E. Dabney)

would have half a bushel of cooked meal and half a bushel of raw meal. Leave it for a couple of days and then go back and mix it up, thin it with stream water and stir it. Then add a couple of gallons of ground corn malt and a gallon of rye meal. Six days later, when the top of the mixture gets clear you have your beer and are ready to run off.

One by one you'd distill each barrel and you'd get six to eight gallons of singlings from each. Then you'd cook them through the still again. That's your doubling run. That's when you get your real alcohol. Be high proof, too high to bead. That's grain alcohol. Those first shots would be 150, 160 proof. As it continues to distill the whiskey proof becomes weaker and when it gets to about 120 proof it will begin to bead. Finally it comes to a good bead, about 100 proof. Corn whiskey has a lot smaller bead than this sugar whiskey nowadays. Sugar puts a big coarse bead on it. Sometime later the whiskey "breaks at the worm", as they say. It starts tasting and smelling sour when it gets to below 90 proof. We call that backings and would put it in with the singlings to be distilled again.

From 50 gallons of singlings I'd expect to get between 16 and 20 gallons of "doubling likker". You'd "fourth" that with about five gallons of stream water giving you about 25 gallons in all. Some folk would cut it with the "backings" but I never did. Cutting with water makes the best likker, .the sweetest tasting. Often the women would say we had it easy up the mountain making moonshine, but let me tell you, we had to really work hard. Ain't no lazy man gonna make the moonshine, it's hard work getting all that stuff up the mountain and avoiding the Revenue men.' There's a lot of men and women in Ireland would echo that.

Postscript on the state of moonshining in America.

The latest figures from the Revenue authorities indicate that over two thirds of the moonshine made today in the USA is made in the cities. In the Appalachians it is now far more profitable for the mountainy men to grow marihuana!

KENTUCKY BOOTLEGGER

Come all you booze buyers if you want to hear
About the kind of booze they sell around here
Made way back in the swamps and hills
Where there's plenty of moonshine stills.

Some moonshiners make pretty good stuff
Bootleggers use it to mix it up
He'll make one gallon, well he'll make two
If you don't mind boys, he'll get the best of you.

One drop will make a rabbit whip a fool dog
And a taste will make a rabbit whip a wild hog
It'll make a toad spit in a black snake's face
Make a hard shell preacher fall from grace.

A lamb will lay down with a lion
After drinking that old moonshine
So throw back your head and take a little drink
And for a week you won't be able to think.

The moonshiners are getting mighty thick
And the bootleggers are getting mighty slick
If they keep on bagging, they better beware
They'll be selling each other I do declare.

MOONSHINER

I've been a moonshiner for seven long years
I make my own whiskey and drink my own beer

I'll go up some hollow and put up a moonshine still
I'll sell you one gallon for a five dollar bill

I'll go to some grocery and I'll drink with my friends
No women to bother to see what I spend

No women to bother no children to squall
If you want to live happy never marry at all

Come all of you pretty women take warning from me
Never lay your affections on a young man like me

BOOTLEGGER'S STORY

Well it's true that the law-men don't like me
They have drove me away from my still
And of course I had to leave there running
Through the wildwood and over the hill

So it's meet me tonight, oh pal meet me
Meet me out in the moonlight alone
For I have ten gallons of good whiskey
Must be sold by the light of the moon

So you see that the officers don't like me
They have drove me away from my door
If I had my time to go over
I would still ten thousand gallons or more

If I knew when the officers were coming
I would be standing in my cabin door
With my pockets full of steel jackets
And a Colt ivory — handled forty - four

Quill Rose, a well known moonshiner from North Carolina on whether it was true that aging improved corn whiskey. 'Your Honour has been misinformed,' replied Quill, 'I have kept some for a week one time and I couldn't tell it was a bit better than when it was new and fresh.'

A surrealist sight in the early morning light. (Irish Times/T.W. Battle)

CHAPTER 5 POITIN IN SONG & STORY

'Philly Cullen, there's a man the peelers are fearing. If you'd that lad in the house there isn't one of them would come smelling round if the dogs themselves were lapping poitin from the dung-pit in the yard.'

J.M. Synge *The Playboy of the Western World*
Reference to poitin are common in the songs, poems and stories of Ireland. What follows is merely a small sample. For stories I have included one of William Carleton's poitin tales. Carleton (1794-1860), from County Tyrone was the son of poor parents who, prevented from becoming a priest, made his way to Dublin and worked for Caesar Otway on the Christian Examiner. His many volumes of tales of the Irish Peasantry are a very useful guide to folk customs and attitudes of the first half of the 19th century, and are much more readable than some of the other Irish writers of the times such as the Bannim brothers or Gerald Griffin. I have also included, by kind permission of Mr Michael McLaverty, his fine short story 'The Poteen Maker'. Frank O'Connor, C.E. Montagu and several other modern authors have also stories about the 'mountain dew' but space, alas! prevents their inclusion.

As for the Irish poems and songs about poitin, I am indebted to Breandán Breathnach and Harry Tipping for their help. I have omitted well known material such as Bó na leathadhairce and chosen to include the less available song 'Bainne Dubh na Féile' and 'Se oakum mo phriosun,' as well as a few old poems about poitin in the Irish tongue.

A wide range of songs about moonshine made my choice difficult but again I ignored such well known material as 'Katie Daly' and included three 20th century songs. Similarly, old favourites such as the 'Jug of Punch' have been omitted and I've included rarer — and much better songs such as 'The Hackler from Grouse Hall' and its sequel 'The Sergeant's Lamentation,' in the selection of Irish songs about poitin in English.

SE OAKHUM MO PHRIOSUN

O'gus molaim su na heornan go deo agus choíchin.
Nach mairg nach mbíonn tóir ag
Rí Seoirse ar a dhéanamh?
Seán Forde a bheith 'na ghiúis tis,
sé chomhairleodh na daoine, mar b'eisean a chuir
ar an eolas dhomsa le oakum a spíonadh.

Is forum de dy dil ó rum, sé oakum mo phríosún,
is gur fhága sú na heornan na hóglaigh dhá spíonadh

'gus maidin ins an tSamhradh is mo leaba déanta
    síos a'm,
d'éirigh mé mo sheasamh nó gur bhreathnaigh mé
    mo thimpeall;
sea chuala mé an hello orm is cén deabhail atá tú
    a dhéanamh,
do dhá láimh in do phócaí 'gus oakum le spíonadh?

    Is foram, etc.

61

Is chuaigh mé féub stór is bhí oakum thar maoil ann;
thug mé lán mo ghabhlach liom, mo dhóthain go
    ceann míosa.
Is nach mise a bhain an gáire as an ngarda a bhí mo
    thimpeall,
Nuair d'fhiaraigh mé den cheannphort arb air a
    d'fhás an fionnach?
    Is foram, etc.

Is nach mise a bhíonn go brónach gach Domhnach
    is lá saoire,
mo sheasamh amuigh san ngairdín istigh i
    bhfáinne's mé goil timpeall?
Is gur sileann ó mo shúile sruth deora nuair
    smaoiním
gurb olc an obair Domhnaigh bheith i gcónaí ar an
    gcaoi seo.
    Is foram, etc.

A Translation

A sad tale of a young man sent to prison to pick
    Oakum for the crime of making poitín.

OAKUM IS MY PRISON

And I praise the juice of the barley for ever and ever.
But isn't it a pity that King George isn't seeking to
    have it made.
And why on earth did someone advise that John
    Forde be made a justice
For it was he who has put me in the way of learning
    to pick oakum!

Chorus:

Is forum de dydilorum, oakum is my prison,
And the young men left the juice of the barley to pick
    it!

And one morning in the summer when I had my bed
    made,

I stood up to have a look around,
And I heard the usual 'what the devil are you doing,
With your hands in your pockets and the oakum not
    picked.'

And I went into the store where the oakum was piled
And I brought out a forkfull, enough for a month
And I made the guards around me laugh
When I asked the commander if the hairy stuff grew
    on *him*

And amn't I the sorry boy every Sunday and holiday,
Standing in the yard or walking the old circle
With the stream of tears pouring down my face
Thinking what a terrible way to be spending a
    Sunday!

BAINNE 'DHUBH NA FÉILE'

Bhí bo-ín bheag agamsa, sé a h-ainm Dubh na Féile.
Ní leagfadh béal ar talamh's thiúbharfadh bainne
    dho na céadta
Dhéanfadh síotcán's cárthannas i Sasana's inÉirinn
Is níor dhóichide sin ná seal eile a' tarraint locaí a
    chéile.

Curfá:

Nó a dtuigeann tú mo chás a bhean an tabhairne a's
    mé glaodhach ort,
Nó a' driúbharfá braon go maidin domh de bhainne
    Dhubh na Féile.
A dóthain a thabhairt le caitheamh di, trí bairillí
    braiche in aenfheacht
Teine a choinnéal faduighth' fúiti is lasair ar gach
    taobh di,
'Sé na dlighthe atá agaibh i Sasana nó in Éirinn
Gach bó dhá dtálann bainne dhóibh, go
    gcoinnigheann siad dóibh féin í.

(Curfá).

An té d'ólfad braon ar maidin di, 's deas a
    mharbhóchadh sé na péiste
Cuirfeadh tinncéaraí 'gus bacaigh a's ceannuidhth'
    a' marbhú a chéile
Sean-mhná, nuair a bhlaiseanns di, a' reic an rud'
    nac ndéarfar,
Agus meidhir an domhain ar shean-daoine a'
    ceapadh gur maith an '**stuf**' dóibh féin é.

(Curfá).

Tá sagairt agus bráithre a' blaiseadh do 'n bhraen úd
An t-easbog is an Pápa, 's ní áirmhighim
    ministéaraí.
Iarlaí 's tighearnaí láidre, gan trácht ar a gcuid
    'ladies'
A's ní fhanócaidís le eadarshuth ach a' bleaghan
    Dubh na Féile.

(Curfá).

Tá lucht "Sequels" agus "Warrants,"
    "Orangemen" a's "Quakers,"
A' tigheacht dho do mharbhú 'sa chlaidhmhe i
    láimh gach aoinneach
Cnaigín a thabhairt do 'n fhear acab ar maidin
    'shdeamhan a' baoghal duit
Agus a chomhursanaí nach beannuighth' an rud é
    bainne Dhubh na Féile.

(Curfá).

Cheannuigh an Róisteach bó ar an aenach,
Trí ghiní óir agus coróin gheal éirnis
Le síorruidheacht na h-aimsire, thuit a taobhannaí
    ó chéile
Agus nar suarach an geáll airgid í maidin lá an
    aenaigh

M. ÓCadhain

A Translation
THE MILK OF THE GENEROUS WEE BLACK COW

I once had a little cow, her name was 'generous
    Blackie.'
She wouldn't put mouth to ground but she'd give
    'milk' to hundreds,
Peace and friendliness she could create between
    England and Ireland,
And you'll have to admit not many could do that!

Chorus:

Oh! Woman of the inn, I beg you help my plight,
Give me some of Blackie's milk, to help me through
    the night.

If you want to give her her fill, why three barrels of
    malt will do,
With a fire kept kindled under her and the flames
    licking all around,
And sure don't the laws of England and Ireland
    allow you
To keep any useful cow that gives you milk.

If you took a drop of it first thing in the morning,
Sure you'd make short work of the snakes.
It would set tinkers, beggars and merchants at each
    other's throats
And old women, when they taste it, would start
    selling things that had never been made.
And old fellows would be on top of the world
    thinking it the quare stuff.

Priests and Brothers are tasting the odd drop,
So are the bishop and Pope, to say nothing of them
    Protestant ministers.
So are the Earls and powerful Lords, not forgetting
    their fancy women
Who'd be out milking 'Generous Blackie' at all times
    of the day!

The 'Sequel' gang, the Warrantmen, Orangemen
    and Quakers,

If they all came to kill you with swords in their hands,
Just give them each a noggin and damn the bit of
    danger you'll be in,
For neighbours, isn't wee Blackie's milk a blessed
    thing!

Didn't the boul' Mr Roche buy a cow at the fair
For three gold guineas and a bright crown as an
    advance.
She'll last till the end of eternity
So wasn't that a good fair-day bargain he got!

M. ÓCadhain

WEST CORK LAMENT FOR PADDY BUCKLEY

Oh rise up Paddy Buckley and come along with me,
And we'll go making whiskey in that place you'd
    long to be,
T'is well you know those mountains where often we
    did stray,
Rise up me boy and come with me at the breaking of
    the day.

And when we're on those hills again t'is there we
    will sit down,
And we'll talk about the raiding and that case in
    Macroom town.
T'was spies and jealous neighbours that gave the
    game away,
But now, thank God, sure we're all safe, on our own
    dear hills again.

When I heard of you being captured, it grieved my
    heart full sore,
To hear you caught the second time, it grieved me
    ten times more,
T'is well I knew that you were true to that gallant
    ancient cause,
Until at last you had to yield to our own cruel Irish
    laws.

One night as I lay sleeping, all in my dreams again,

I thought I saw him standing on yon green heathery
    hill,
I thought I heard him singing by that lovely rippling
    rill
Where many a time in days of yore t'was there we
    drank our fill.

One dark night last December I heard an old man
    say,
Was it true that he was captured or did he get away?
All those mountains look so lonely since from them
    he did go,
O Gradh mo croidhe I'd love to see him pass this way
    once more.

When I hear the people talking it grieves me deep to
    hear
That Buckley now his race is run and to some foreign
    shore he'll steer
But I'll always contradict them, knowing him since
    the days of old,
He's happier on that mountain than a king upon his
    throne.

Now to conclude and finish for my pen is running
    dry,
There is an old sean-fhocal that old soldiers never
    die,
So when Christmas comes around again with him I'd
    long to be,
And we'll stroll down some high mountain with a jar
    of grand poitin.

Irish piper. (Lawrence Collection, National Library of Ireland)

IRISH PIPER 6930W

CRUISCÍN LÁN

Oh come all you lads and lassies, pray attend to my
  oration,
I hope you'll hear me in my song and give me an
  ovation,
I now intend your voices and your kindly
  concentration,
To wish me joy and happiness in sport and
  transportation,
Is gheomaris an cruiscan is biodh se lan.

It was in the month of June or so some cowardly
  hearted traitor,
He went into the barracks and his story there
  related,
He said that in a Western glen far, far out in the
  mountains,
There was a poitin Irish still, flowing from a crystal
  fountain.

It was early the next morning, the police made
  preparations,
They hired a car and driver, for to take them to this
  station,
But when they reached the shanty, they found they
  were mistaken,
There was neither manufacturer nor anything
  relating.

Now that crystal drop flowing from the still, t'would
  cure all sorts of ailments,
T'would cure the yellow jaundice, both the scarletine
  and measles,
T'would banish heart diseases, from your lungs
  would drive flammation,
From your soul t'would drive the Devil, from your
  heart t'would drive temptation.

Now that Christmas is approaching boys, we're in a
  consternation,
We don't know where to get a drop, without
  adulteration,
Our local manufacture is the finest in the nation,
And of course it is distributed, without duty or
  taxation.

And now to conclude and finish, and I hope I've said
  no traison,
Freedom is soon dawning and we'll have home rule
  in Erin,
We'll banish all land grabbers and cowardly hearted
  traitors,
We'll have our poitin Irish still, annsúd gan
  buiochas d'einne.

POTEEN GOOD LUCK TO YE, DEAR!

Av I was a monarch in state,
Like Romulus or Julius Caysar,
With the best of fine victuals to eat,
And drink like great Nebuchadnezzar,
A rasher of bacon I'd have,
And potatoes the finest was seen, sir;
And for drink, it's no claret I'd crave,
But a keg of ould Mullen's potheen, sir,
With the smell of the smoke on it still.

They talk of the Romans of ould,
Whom, they say, in their own times was frisky,
But trust me to keep out of the cowld,
The Romans at home here like whiskey.
Sure it warms both the head and the heart,
It's the soul of all readin' and writin';
It teaches both science and art,
And disposes for love or for fightin'.
Oh! potteen, good luck to ye, dear!

Charles Lever

THE HACKLER FROM GROUSE HALL

I am a rovin' hackler lad that loves the shamrock
  shore,
My name is Pat McDonnell and my age is eighty-
  four,
Belov'd and well repected by my neighbours one and
  all,
On Saint Patrick's Day I loved to stray round Lavey
  and Grouse Hall.

When I was young I danced and sung and drank
  good whiskey, too,
Each shebeen shop that sold a drop of the real old
  mountain dew
With the poteen still on every hill the peelers had no
  call
Round sweet Stradone I am well known, round Lavey
  and Grouse Hall.

I rambled round from town to town for hackling was
  my trade
None can deny I think that I an honest living made
Where'ere I'd stay by night or day the youth would
  always call
To have some crack with Paddy Jack the Hackler
  from Grouse Hall.

I think it strange how times have changed so very
  much of late
Coercion now is all the row and Peelers on their bate
To take a glass is now alas the greatest crime of all
Since Balfour placed that hungry beast the Sergeant
  of Grouse Hall.

The busy tool of Castle rule he travels night and day
He'll seize a goat just by the throat for want of better
  prey
The nasty skunk he'll swear you're drunk tho' you
  took none at all
There is no peace about the place since he came to
  Grouse Hall.

'Twas on pretence of this offence he dragged me off
  to jail
Alone to dwell in a cold cell my fate for to bewail;
My hoary head on a plank bed such wrongs for
  vengeance call
He'll rue the day he dragged away the Hackler from
  Grouse Hall.

He haunts the League, just like a plague, and shame
  for to relate
The Priest can't be on Sunday free the Mass to
  celebrate;
It's there he'll kneel encased in steel prepared on
  duty's call
For to assail and drag to jail our clergy from Grouse
  Hall,
Down into hell he'd run pellmell to hunt for poteen
  there
And won't be loth to swear an oath 'twas found in
  Killinkere.
He'll search your bed from foot to head, sheets,
  blankets, tick and all
You wife undressed must leave the nest for Jemmy
  of Grouse Hall.

He fixed a plan for that poor man who had a
  handsome wife
To take away without delay her liberty and life
He'd swear quite plain that he's insane and got no
  sense at all
As he has done of late with one convenient to Grouse
  Hall.

His raid on dogs I'm sure it flogs it's shocking to
  behold
How he'll pull up a six month's pup and swear it's a
  two year old;
Outside of hell a parallel can't be found for him at all
For that vile pimp and devil's imp the ruler of
  Grouse Hall.

Each loyal man if such there can be found about
   Grouse Hall
Come join with me in sympathy and pity my
   downfall,
I am despised and stigmatised for tyranny and
   wrong
Both far and near my name you'll hear re-echoed on
   a song.

I am belied because I tried to enforce the law
And keep the peace around the place with drunken
   roughs and all
Tho' my protest may be expressed in language
   rather strong
I think I'm bound for to confound the author of that
   song.

That hackling clown who can let down a tear with
   every smile
And all his days with perfect ease could act the
   crocodile
With nimble shanks he plays his pranks on peelers
   all along
And does aim to blast my fame by his wild rebel
   song.

He begs along and sings a song and has no care at all
And all around the hills resound with Jemmy of
   Grouse Hall;
But very soon he'll change his tune with bolts of iron
   strong
When Balfour's shears gets round his ears he'll sing
   another song.

The league 'tis true I did pursue the priest why
   should I spare
Who broke the laws and was the cause of bloodshed
   everywhere

But Martin's fall in Donegal will be avenged ere long
McFadden's crew will get their due then who will
   sing the song.

I do deny that ever I a naked female seen
The gentle sex I know they're vexed they fell the
   insult keen.
It was a shame to fix such blame upon me in the
   wrong
But while I live I'll not forgive the man that made the
   song.

In all my life to Tully's wife I never spoke a word
The crazy loon cried out too soon his jealous mind
   was stirred
I still maintain that he's insane tho' Lovelock says
   I'm wrong
That mental quack I'm told for fact 'twas he who
   made the song.

My poteen raid I am afraid 'twill end in failure too
Attorney Lynch won't yield an inch in what he does
   pursue.
The logic sound can well confound my cases right
   and wrong
No doubt but he might chance to be the man that
   made the song.

There's men of course among the force who
   sympathise with me
There's others, too, but not a few can well enjoy the
   spree.
To them I say a reckoning day will come before its
   long
And Cooper's fate will compensate the man that
   sings the song.

I'll give five pounds and jink it down to find the
   poet's name
Because, of course, he is the source of all my grief
   and shame.

And in a coach to Cecil Roche I'll march him through
    the throng
I know he'll be right glad to see the man that made
    the song.

In all my boast the hackler's ghost annoys me most
    of all
I'm still in dread that when he's dead he'll haunt me
    from Grouse Hall
In dreams at night I rave and fright in accents shrill
    and long
That pierce my ears I think I hear the echo of his
    song.

I'm well content for to be sent away this very day
To Cork or Clare or anywhere one hundred miles
    away.
This curst Grouse Hall caused my downfall I have
    been here too long
Before I'd go I'd wish to know the man that made the
    song.

NOTES

'Hackler': In the days of this ballad a lot of flax was
grown in Co. Cavan. The people prepared their own
flax and made it into thread for use on the spinning
wheels. The last operation prior to the flax being
made ready for spinning was called 'hackling.' It
was a process of fining down the flax in preparation
for the spinning wheel. Hackling was a trade and
hacklers went from house to house hackling the flax
in each house.

Reference to Celebration of Mass in the 'Hackler'
and to Martin and McFadden in 'The Sergeant's
Lamentation': Father McFadden of Glenties, Co.
Donegal, made a seditious speech in favour of the
Land League. A special force of police was brought
to Donegal to arrest him, among them the Grouse
Hall Sergeant. The force was under D.I. Martin. On
Sunday morning during Mass the police surrounded
the chapel and arrested Father McFadden
immediately after Mass. The people who were at
Mass congregated around and a melée ensued in
which D.I. Martin was killed. The affair got great
publicity but it was never discovered who was
responsible for Martin's death.

Searching of Beds: The people used to hide the
poteen in the bed, and the Sergeant always search
the beds. Attorney Lynch was a Solicitor in Virginia
who always defended the people in poteen
prosecutions.

Balfour's Shears: Reference to the close crop given
to convicts. Balfour was Secretary for Ireland
1887—91.

Cooper: Probably a member of the R.I.C. who was
dismissed.

Words and notes supplied by John Smith, Stravic-
nabo, Ballyjamesduff, Co. Cavan.

A COUNTY TYRONE POITIN FOLK TALE

The incident related here happened in the 1820s at
Doons, a townland five miles to the West of
Cookstown. It appears in Munterloney Folk Tales
collected by Eamonn O'Tuathail and published by
the Irish Folklore Institute in Dublin in 1933. This
translation from the Irish is by Harry Tipping.
   'About Christmas time here the weather was
rather wet and stormy. It was difficult to do
anything. Christmas Eve was a busy day for me. I
rose early in the morning and went out and cleaned
all the outhouses and sheds, gave the cattle their
fodder then went into the field and brought in the
wether (castrated ram) to be killed for Christmas.
And the wife says to me, ''we're grand now, but
we've nothing to drink as we should have at
Christmas.''

"We'll not be long like that," says I, "for I'll go down to the pub in Doons and I'll get two quarts of poitin and that will do ourselves and any on the neighbours that we want to give a drop to."

So I went down to the pub and the yard and the house itself were full of people. They were all agog with the news that the big millstone from Doons Mill had been stolen the previous night and nobody knew who had taken it. Well, the police had been called and they were on their way when they met a woman called Peggy from Doons, and didn't Big Peggy have the millstone hidden under her cloak. And when she saw them she took off with them trying to catch her and over the hills she went with the stone and dropped it in Lough Fea. Back she comes and there was nothing anyone could prove.

So we're all drinking in the pub and talking about this when in walks Big Peggy herself. And the miller says to her, "If you bring that millstone back I'll give you a quart of poitin, for it would be difficult to find the men that could find a stone in the lake and get it out."

"Right", says she, and off she goes to Lough Fea, jumps into the water, rolls out the great big stone and brings it back to its stand at the mill. Then in she comes and the miller and everyone laughing and cheering and the quart of poitin was reached to her and we all began to talk about all the great feats of strength Big Peggy had done. And she passed the poitin around for all to drink and one quart led to another until they all had their fill. Then they started on the dancing and Peggy was dancing too. And if you'd seen that woman dancing! She would shake the loft! No three men were as strong as she was. Boys, did I go home happy that night!

Up in the morning early and off to Mass. And when we came back we invited a few of the neighbours in and we had the two quarts of poitin and all in all we had some crack that Christmas.'

BOB PENTLAND

That the Irish are a ready-witted people, is a fact to the truth of which testimony has been amply borne both by their friends and enemies. Many causes might be brought forward to account for this questionable gift, if it were our intention to be philosophical; but as the matter has been so generally conceded, it would be but a waste of logic to prove to the world that which the world cares not about, beyond the mere fact that it is so. On this or any other topic one illustration is worth twenty arguments, and, accordingly, instead of broaching a theory we shall relate a story.

Behind the hill or rather mountain of Altnaveenan lies one of those deep and almost precipitous valleys, on which the practised eye of an illicit distiller would dwell with delight, as a topography not likely to be invaded by the unhallowed feet of the gauger and his red-coats. In point of fact, the spot we speak of was from its peculiarly isolated situation nearly invisible, unless to such as came very close to it. Being so completely hemmed in and concealed by the round and angular projections of the mountain hills, you could never dream of its existence at all, until you came upon the very verge of the little precipitous gorge which led into it. This advantage of position was not, however, its only one. It is true indeed that the moment you had entered it, all possibility of its being applied to the purposes of distillation at once vanished, and you consequently could not help exclaiming, 'what a pity that so safe and beautiful a nook should have not a single spot on which to erect a still-house, or rather on which to raise a sufficient stream of water to the elevation necessary for the process of distilling.' If a gauger actually came to the little chasm, and cast his scrutinizing eye over it, he would immediately perceive that the erection of a private still in such a place was a piece of folly not generally to be found in the plans of those who have recourse to such practices.

This absence, however, of the requisite conveniences was only apparent, not real. To the right, about one hundred yards above the entrance to it, ran a ledge of rocks, some fifty feet high, or so. Along the lower brows, near the ground, grew thick matted masses of long heath, which covered the entrance to a cave about as large and as high as an ordinary farm-house. Through a series of small fissures in the rocks which formed its roof, descended a stream of clear soft water, precisely in body and volume such as was actually required by the distiller; but, unless by lifting up this mass of heath, no human being could for a moment imagine that there existed any such grotto, or so unexpected and easy an entrance to it. Here there was a private still-house made by the hand of nature herself, such as no art or ingenuity of man could equal.

Now it so happened that about the period we write of, there lived in our parish two individuals so antithetical to each other in their pursuits of life, that we question whether throughout all the instinctive antipathies of nature we could find any two animals more destructive of each other than the two we mean —to wit, Bob Pentland, the gauger, and little George Steen, the illicit distiller. Pentland was an old, stanch, well-trained fellow, of about fifty years or more, steady and sure, and with all the characteristic points of the high-bred gauger about him. He was a tallish man, thin but lathy, with a hooked nose that could scent the tread of a distiller with the keeness of a slew-hound; his dark eye was deep-set, circumspect, and roguish in its expression, and his shaggy brow seemed always to be engaged in calculating whereabouts his inveterate foe, little George Steen, that eternally blinked him, when almost in his very fangs, might then be distilling. To be brief, Pentland was proverbial for his sagacity and adroitness in detecting distillers, and little George was equally proverbial for having always baffled him, and that, too, sometimes under circumstances, where escape seemed hopeless.

The incidents which we are about to detail occurred at that period of time when the collective wisdom of our legislators thought it advisable to impose a fine upon the whole townland in which the Still, Head and Worm, might be found; thus opening a door for knavery and fraud, and, as it proved in most cases, rendering the innocent as liable to suffer for an offence they never contemplated, as the guilty who planned and perpetrated it. The consequence of such a law was, that still-houses were always certain to be erected either at the very verge of the neighbouring districts, or as near them as the circumstances of convenience and situation would permit. The moment of course that the hue-and-cry of the gauger and his myrmidons were heard upon the wind, the whole apparatus was immediately heaved over the mering to the next townland, from which the fine imposed by parliament was necessarily raised, whilst the crafty and offending district actually escaped. The state of society generated by such a blundering and barbarous statute as this, was dreadful. In the course of a short time, reprisals, law-suits, battles, murders and massacres, multipled to such an extent throughout the whole country, that the sapient senators who occasioned such commotion were compelled to repeal their own act as soon as they found how it worked. Necessity, together with being the mother of invention, is also the cause of many an accidental discovery.

Pentland had been so frequently defeated by little George, that he vowed never to rest until he had secured him; and George on the other hand frequently told him — for they were otherwise on the best terms — that he defied him, or as he himself more quaintly expressed it, 'that he defied the devil, the world, and Bob Pentland.' The latter, however, was a very sore thorn in his side, and drove him from place to place, and from one haunt to another, until he began to despair of being able any longer to outwit him, or to find within the parish any spot at all suitable for distillation with which Pentland was not acquainted. In this state stood matters between them, when George fortunately discovered at the hip of Altnaveenan hill the natural grotto we have just sketched so briefly. Now, George was a man, as we have already hinted, of great fertility of resources; but there existed in the same parish another distiller who outstripped him in that far-sighted cunning which is so necessary in misleading or circumventing such a sharp-scented old hound as Pentland. This was little Mickey M'Quade, a short-necked squat little fellow with bow legs, who might be said rather to creep in his motion than to walk. George and Mickey were intimate friends, independently of their joint antipathy against the gauger, and, truth to tell, much of the mortification and many of the defeats which Pentland experienced at George's hands, were *sub rosa* to be attributed to Mickey. George was a distiller from none of the motives which generally actuate others of that class. He was in truth an analytic philosopher — a natural chemist never out of some new experiment — and we have reason to think he might have been the Kane, or Faraday, or Dalton, of his day, had he only received a scientific education. Not so honest Mickey, who never troubled his head about an experiment, but only thought of making a good running, and defeating the gauger. The first thing of course that George did, was to consult Mickey, and both accordingly took a walk up to the scene of their future operations. On examining it, and fully perceiving its advantages, it might well be said that the look of exultation and triumph which passed between them was not unworthy of their respective characters.

'This will do,' said George. 'Eh—don't you think we'll put our finger in Pentland's eye yet?' Mickey spat sagaciously over his beard, and after a second glance gave one grave grin which spoke volumes. 'It'll do,' said he; 'but there's one point to be got over that maybe you didn't think of; an' you know that half a blink, half a point, is enough for Pentland.'

'What is it?'

'What do you intend to do with the smoke when the fire's lit? There'll be no keepin' *that* down. Let Pentland see but as much smoke risin' as would come out of an ould woman's dudeen, an' he'd have us.'

George started, and it was clear by the vexation and disappointment which were visible on his brow that unless this untoward circumstance could be managed, their whole plan was deranged, and the cave of no value.

'What's to be done?' he inquired of his cooler companion.

'If we can't get over this, we may bid good bye to it.'

'Never mind,' said Mickey; 'I'll manage it, and *do* Pentland still.' 'Ay, but how?'

'It's no matter. Let us not lose a minute in settin' to work. Lave the other thing to me; an' if I don't account for the smoke without discoverin' the entrance to the still, I'll give you lave to crop the ears off my head.'

George knew the cool but steady self-confidence for which Mickey was remarkable, and accordingly, without any further interrogatory, they both proceeded to follow up their plan of operations.

In those times when distillation might be truly considered as almost universal, it was customary for farmers to build their out-houses with secret chambers and other requisite partitions necessary for carrying it on. Several of them had private stores built between false walls, the entrance to which was only known to a few, and many of them had what were called *Malt-steeps* sunk in hidden recesses and hollow gables, for the purpose of steeping the barley, and afterwards of turning and airing it, until it was sufficiently hard to be kiln-dried and ground. From the mill it was usually conveyed to the still-house upon what were termed *Slipes* a kind of car that was made without wheels, in order the more easily to pass through morasses and bogs which no wheeled vehicle could encounter.

In the course of a month or so, George and Mickey, aided by their friends, had all the apparatus of keeve, hogshead, &c., together with Still, Head, and Worm, set up and in full work.

'And now Mickey', inquired his companion, 'how will you manage about the smoke? for you know that the two worst informers against a private distiller, barrin' a *stag* is a smoke by day an' a fire by night.'

'I know that', replied Mickey; 'an' a rousin' smoke we'll have, for fraid a little puff wouldn't do us. Come, now, an' I'll show you.'

They both ascended to the top, where Mickey had closed all the open fissures of the roof with the exception of that which was directly over the fire of the still. This was at best not more than six inches in breadth, and about twelve long. Over it he placed a piece of strong plate-iron perforated with holes, and on this he had a fire of turf, beside which sat a little boy who acted as a vidette. The thing was simple but effective. Clamps of turf were at every side of them, and the boy was instructed, if the gauger, whom he well knew, ever appeared, to heap on fresh fuel, so as to increase the smoke in such a manner as to induce him to suppose that *all* he saw of it proceeded merely from the fire before him. In fact, the smoke from the cave below was so completely identified with and lost in that which was emitted from the fire above, that no human being could penetrate the mystery, if not made previously acquainted with it. The writer of this saw it during the hottest process of distillation, and failed to make the discovery, although told that the still-house was within a circle of three hundred yards, the point he stood on being considered the centre. On more than one occasion has he absconded from home, and spent a whole night in the place, seized with that indescribable fascination which such a scene holds forth to youngsters, as well as from his irrepressible anxiety to hear the old stories and legends with the recital of which they generally pass the night.

In this way, well provided against the gauger — indeed much better than our readers are yet aware of, as they shall understand by and bye — did George, Mickey, and their friends, proceed for the greater part of a winter without a single visit from Pentland. Several successful runnings had come off, which had of course turned out highly profitable, and they were just now preparing to commence their last, not only for the season, but the last they should ever work together, as George was making preparations to go early in the spring to America. Even this running was going on to their satisfaction, and the singlings had been thrown again into the still, from the worm of which projected the strong medicinal *first-shot* as the doubling commenced — this last term meaning the spirit in its pure and finished state. On this occasion the two worthies were more than ordinarily anxious, and certainly doubled their usual precautions against a surprise, for they knew that Pentland's visits resembled the pounces of a hawk or the springs of a tiger more than any thing else to which they could compare them. In this they were not disappointed. When the doubling was about half finished, he made his appearance, attended by a strong party of reluctant soldiers — for indeed it is due to the military to state that they never took delight in harassing the country people at

the command of a keg-hunter, as they generally nicknamed the gauger. It had been arranged that the vidette at the iron plate should whistle a particular tune the moment that the gauger or a red-coat, or in fact any person whom he did not know, should appear. Accordingly, about eight o'clock in the morning they heard the little fellow in his highest key whistling up that well-known and very significant old Irish air called 'Go to the devil an' shake yourself' — which in this case was applied to the gauger in any thing but an allegorical sense.

'Be the pins,' which was George's usual oath, 'be the pins, Mickey, it's over with us — Pentland's here, for there's the sign.'

Mickey paused for a moment and listened very gravely; then squirting out a tobacco spittle, 'Take it aisy', said he; 'I have half a dozen fires about the hills, any one as like this as your right hand is to your left. I didn't spare trouble, for I knew that if we'd get over *this* day, we'd be out of his power.'

'Well, my good lad,' said Pentland, addressing the vidette, 'what's this fire for?'

'What is it for, is it?'

'Yes, if you don't let me know instantly, I'll blow your brains out, and get you hanged and transported afterwards.' This he said with a thundering voice, cocking a large horse pistol at the same time.

'Why sir,' said the boy, 'it's watchin' a still I am; but be the hole o' my coat if you tell upon me, it's broilin' upon these coals I'll be soon.'

'Where is the still then? An' the still-house, where is it?'

'Oh, begorra, as to where the still or still-house is, they wouldn't tell *me* that.'

'Why, sirra, didn't you say this moment you were watching a still?'

'I meant, sir', replied the lad, with a face that spoke of pure idiocy, 'that it was the gauger I was watchin', an' I was to whistle upon my fingers to let the boy at that fire on the hill there above know that he was comin'.'

'Who told you to do so?'

'Little George, sir, an' Mickey M'Quade.'

'Ay, ay, right enough there, my lad — two of the most notorious schemers unhanged they are both. But now, like a good boy, tell me the truth, an' I'll give you the price of a pair of shoes. Do you know where the still or still-house is? Because if you do, an' won't tell me, here are the soldiers at hand to make a prisoner of you; an' if they do, all the world can't prevent you from being hanged, drawn, and quartered.'

'Oh, bad cess may seize the morsel o' me knows that; but if you'll give me the money, sir, I'll tell you who can bring you to it, for he tould me yesterday mornin' that he knew, an' offered to bring me there last night, if I'd steal him a bottle that my mother keeps the holy water in at home, tal he'd put whiskey in it.'

'Well, my lad, who is this boy?'

'Do you know "Harry Neil, or Mankind," sir?'

'I do, my good boy.'

'Well, it's a son of his, sir; an' look, sir: do you see the smoke farthest up to the right, sir?'

'To the right? Yes,'

'Well, 'tis there, sir, that Darby Neil is watchin'; and he *says* he knows.'

'How long have you been watching here?'

'This is only the third day, sir, for *me* but the rest, them boys above, has been here a good while.'

'Have you seen nobody stirring about the hills since you came?'

'Only once, sir, yestherday, I seen two men, havin' an empty sack or two, runnin' across the hill there above.'

At this moment the military came up, for he had himself run forward in advance of them, and he repeated the substance of his conversation with our friend the vidette. Upon examining the stolidity of his countenance, in which there certainly was a woeful deficiency of meaning, they agreed among themselves that his appearance justified the truth of the story which he told the gauger, and upon being still further interrogated, they were confirmed that none but a stupid lout like himself would entrust to his keeping any secret worth knowing. They now separated themselves into as many detached parties as there were fires burning on the hills about them, the gauger himself resolving to make for that which Darby Neil had in his keeping, for he could not help thinking that the vidette's story was too natural to be false. They were just in the act of separating themselves to pursue their different routes, when the lad said,

'Look, sir! bad scran be from me but there's a still any way. Sure I often seen a still: that's just like the one that Philip Hogan the tinker mended in George Steen's barn.'

'Hollo, boys', exclaimed Pentland, 'stoop! stoop! they are coming this way, and don't see us: no, hang them, no! they have discovered us now, and are off towards Mossfield. By Jove this will be a bitter trick if they succeed; confound them, they are bent for Ballagh, which is my own property; and may I be hanged but if we do not intercept them it is I myself who will have to pay the fine.'

The pursuit instantly commenced with a speed and vigour equal to the ingenuity of this singular act of retaliation on the gauger. Pentland himself being long-winded from much practice in this way, and being further stimulated by the prospective loss which he dreaded, made as beautiful a run of it as any man of his years could do. It was all in vain, however. He merely got far enough to see the Still, Head, and Worm, heaved across the march ditch into his own property, and to reflect after seeing it that he was certain to have the double consolation of being made a standing joke of for life, and of paying heavily for the jest out of his own pocket. In the mean time, he was bound of course to seize the still, and report the capture; and as he himself farmed the townland in question, the fine was levied to the last shilling, upon the very natural principle that if he had been sufficiently active and vigilant, no man would have attempted to set up a still so convenient to his own residence and property.

This manoeuvre of keeping in reserve an old or second set of apparatus, for the purpose of acting the lapwing and misleading the gauger, was afterwards often practised with success; but the first discoverer of it was undoubtedly Mickey M'Quade, although the honour of the discovery is attributed to his friend George Steen. The matter, however, did not actually end here, for in a few days afterwards some malicious wag — in other words, George himself — had correct information sent to Pentland touching the locality of the cavern and the secret of its entrance. On this occasion the latter brought a larger military party than usual along with him, but it was only to make him feel that he stood in a position if possible still more ridiculous than the first. He found indeed the marks of recent distillation in the place, but nothing else. Every vessel and implement connected with the process had been removed, with the exception of one bottle of whiskey, to which was attached by a bit of twine the following friendly note:—

'Mr. PENTLAND, SIR — Take this bottle home and drink your own health. You can't do less. It was distilled *under your nose* the first day you came to look for us, and bottled for you while you were speaking to the little boy that made a hare of you. Being distilled then under your nose, let it be drunk in the same place, and don't forget while doing so to drink the health of   G.S.'

The incident went abroad like wildfire, and was known everywhere. Indeed for a long time it was the standing topic of the parish; and so sharply was it felt by Pentland that he could never keep his temper if asked, 'Mr. Pentland, when did you see little George Steen?' — a question to which he was never known to give a civil reply.

William Carlton

The poitín maker. 'Just a wee sip…
(*Irish Times/T. W. Battle*)

Too much? (Irish Times/T. W. Battle)

THE POTEEN MAKER

When he taught me some years ago, he was an old man near his retirement, and when he would pass through the streets of the little town on his way from school, you would hear the women talking about him as they stood at their doors knitting or nursing their babies: 'Poor man, he's done . . . Killing himself . . . Digging his own grave!' With my bag of books under my arm I could hear them, but I could never understand why they said he was digging his own grave, and when I would ask my mother, she would scold me: 'Take your dinner like a good boy, and don't be listening to the hard back-biters of this town. Your father has always a good word for Master Craig — so that should be enoughfor you!'

'But why do they say he's killing himself?'

'Why do who say? Didn't I tell you to take your dinner and not be repeating what the idle gossips of this town are saying? Listen to me, son! Master Craig is a decent, good-living man — a kindly man that would go out of his way to do you a good turn. If Master Craig was in any other town, he'd have got a place in the new school at the Square instead of being stuck for ever in that wee poky bit of a school at the edge of the town!'

It was true that the school was small — a two-roomed ramshackle of a place that lay at the edge of the town beyond the last street lamp. We all loved it. Around it grew a few trees, their trunks hacked with boys' names and pierced with nibs and rusty drawing-pins. In summer, when the windows were open we could hear the leaves rubbing together and in winter, see the raindrops hanging on the bare twigs.

It was a draughty place and the master was always complaining of the cold, and even in the early autumn he would wear his overcoat in the classroom and rub his hands together: 'Boys, it's very cold today. Do you feel it cold?' And to please him, we would answer: 'Yes, sir, 'tis very cold.' He would continue to rub his hands, and he would look at the old trees casting their leaves or at the broken spout that flung its tail of rain against the window. He always kept his hands clean and three times a day he would wash them in a basin and wipe them on a roller towel affixed to the inside of his press. He had a hanger for his coat and a brush to brush away the chalk that accumulated on the collar in the course of the day.

In the wet, windy month of November, three buckets were placed on the top of the decks to catch the drips that plopped here and there from the ceiling, and those drops made different music according to the direction of the wind. When the buckets were filled, the master always called me to empty them, and I would take them one at a time and swirl them into the drain at the street and stand for a minute gazing down at the wet roofs of the town or listen to the rain pecking at the lunch-papers scattered about on the cinders.

'What's it like outside?' he always asked when I came in with the empty buckets.

'Sir, 'tis very bad.'

He would write sums on the board and tell me to keep an eye on the class, and out to the porch he would go and stand in grim silence watching the rain nibbling at the puddles. Sometimes he would come in and I would see him sneak his hat from the press and disappear for five or ten minutes. We would fight then with rulers or paper-darts till our noise would disturb the mistress next door and in she would come and stand with her lips compressed, her finger in her book. There was silence as she upbraided us: 'Mean, low, good-for-nothing corner boys. Wait'll Mister Craig comes back and I'll let him know the angels he has. And I'll give him special news about *you*' — and she shakes her book at me: 'An altar boy on Sunday and a corner boy for the rest of the week!' We would let her barge away, the buckets plink-plonking as they filled up with rain and her own class beginning to hum, now that she was away from them.

When Mr. Craig came back he would look at us and ask if we disturbed Miss Lagan. Our silence or our tossed hair always gave him the answer. He would correct the sums on the board, flivell the pages of a book with his thumb, and listen to us reading; and occasionally he would glance out of the side-window at the river that flowed through the town and, above it, the bedraggled row of houses whose tumbling yardwalls sheered to the water's edge. 'The loveliest county in Ireland is County Down!' he used to say, with a sweep of his arm to the river and the tin cans and the chalked walls of the houses.

During that December he was ill for two weeks and when he came back amongst us, he was greatly failed. To keep out the draughts he nailed perforated plywood over the ventilators and stuffed blotting paper between the wide crevices at the jambs of the door. There were muddy marks of a ball on one of the windows and on one pane a long crack with fangs at the end of it: 'So someone has drawn the River Ganges while I was away,' he said; and whenever he came to the geography of India, he would refer to the Ganges delta by pointing to the cracks on the pane.

When our ration of coal for the fire was used up, he would send me into the town with a bucket, a coat over my head to keep off the rain, and the money in my fist to buy a stone of coal. He always gave me a penny to buy sweets for myself, and I can always remember that he kept his money in a waistcoat pocket. Back again I would come with the coal and he would give me disused exercise books to light the fire. 'Chief stoker!' he called me, and the name has stuck to me to this day.

It was at this time that the first snow had fallen, and someone by using empty potato bags had climbed over the glass-topped wall and stolen the school coal, and for some reason Mr. Craig did not send me with the bucket to buy more. The floor was continually wet from our boots, and our breaths frosted the windows. Whenever the door opened, a cold draught would rush in and gulp down the breath-warmed air in the room. We would jig our feet and sit on our hands to warm them. Every half-hour Mr. Craig would make us stand and while he lilted *O'Donnell Abu*, we did a series of physical exercises which he had taught us, and in the excitement and the exaltation, we forgot about our sponging boots and the snow that pelted against the windows. It was then that he did his lessons on Science; and we were delighted to see the bunsen burner attached to the gas bracket which hung like an inverted T from the middle of the ceiling. The snoring bunsen seemed to heat up the room and we all gathered round it, pressing in on top of it till he scattered us back to our places with the cane: 'Sit down!' he would shout. 'There's no call to stand. Everybody will be able to see!'

The cold spell remained, and over and over again he repeated one lesson in Science, which he called: *Evaporation and Condensation*.

'I'll show you how to purify the dirtiest of water,' he had told us. 'Even the filthiest water from the old river could be made fit for drinking purposes.' In a glass trough he had a dark brown liquid and when I got his back turned, I dipped my finger in it and it tasted like treacle or burnt candy, and then I remembered about packets of brown sugar and tins of treacle I had seen in his press.

He placed some of the brown liquid in a glass retort and held it aloft to the class: 'In the retort I have water which I have discoloured and made impure. In a few minutes I'll produce from it the clearest of spring water.' And his weary eyes twinkled, and although we could see nothing funny in that, we smiled because he smiled.

The glass retort was set up with the flaming bunsen underneath, and as the liquid was boiling, the steam was trapped in a long-necked flask on which I sponged cold water. With our eyes we followed the bubbling mixture and the steam turning into drops and dripping rapidly into the flask. The air was filled with a biscuity smell, and the only sound was the snore of the bunsen. Outside was the cold air and the falling snow. Presently the master turned out the gas and held up the flask containing the clear water.

'As pure as crystal!' he said, and we watched him pour some of it into a tumbler, hold it in his delicate fingers, and put it to his lips. With wonder we watched him drink it and then our eyes travelled to the dirty, cakey scum that had congealed on the glass sides of the retort. He pointed at this with his ruler: 'The impurities are sifted out and the purest of pure water remains.' And for some reason he gave his roguish smile. He filled up the retort again with the dirty brown liquid and repeated the experiment until he had a large bottle filled with the purest of pure water.

The following day it was still snowing and very cold. The master filled up the retort with the clear liquid which he had stored in the bottle: 'I'll boil this again to show you that there are no impurities left.' So once again we watched the water bubbling, turning to steam, and then to shining drops. Mr. Craig filled up his tumbler: 'As pure as crystal,' he said, and then the door opened and in walked the Inspector. He was muffled to the ears and snow covered his hat and his attaché case. We all stared at him — he was the old, kind man whom we had seen before. He glanced at the bare firegrate and at the closed windows with their sashes edged with snow.

The water continued to bubble in the retort, giving out its pleasant smell.

The Inspector shook hands with Mr. Craig and they talked and smiled together, the Inspector now and again looking towards the empty grate and shaking his head. He unrolled his scarf and flicked the snow from off his shoulders and from his attaché case. He sniffed the air, rubbed his frozen hands together, and took a black notebook from his case. The snow ploffed against the windows and the wind hummed under the door.

'Now, boys', Mr. Craig continued, holding up the tumbler of water from which a thread of steam wriggled in the air. He talked to us in a strange voice and told us about the experiment as if we were seeing it for the first time. Then the Inspector took the warm tumbler and questioned us on our lesson. 'It should be perfectly pure water', he said, and he sipped at it. He tasted its flavour. He sipped at it again. He turned to Mr. Craig. They whispered together, the Inspector looking towards the retort which was still bubbling and sending out its twirls of steam to be condensed to water of purest crystal. He laughed loudly, and we smiled when he again put the tumbler to his lips and his time drank it all. Then he asked us more questions and told us how, if we were shipwrecked, we could make pure water from the salt sea water.

Mr. Craig turned off the bunsen and the Inspector spoke to him. The master filled up the Inspector's tumbler and poured out some for himelf in a cup. Then the Inspector made jokes with us, listened to us singing, and told us we were the best class in Ireland. Then he gave us a few sums to do in our books. He put his hands in his pockets and jingled his money, rubbed a little peep-hole in the breath-covered window and peered out at the loveliest sight in Ireland. He spoke to Mr. Craig again and Mr. Craig shook hands with him and they both laughed.

The Inspector looked at his watch. Our class was let out early, and while I remained behind to tidy up the Science apparatus the master gave me an empty treacle tin to throw in the bin and told me to carry the Inspector's case up to the station. I remember that day well as I walked behind them through the snow, carrying the attaché case, and how loudly they talked and laughed as the snow whirled cold from the river. I remember how they crouched together to light their cigarettes, how match after match was thrown on the road, and how they walked off with the unlighed cigarettes still in their mouths. At the station, Mr. Craig took a penny from his waistcoat pocket and as he handed it to me, it dropped on the snow. I lifted it and he told me I was the best boy in Ireland …

When I was coming from his funeral last week — God have mercy on him — I recalled that wintry day and the feel of the cold penny and how much more I know now about Mr. Craig than I did then. On my way out of the town — I don't live there now — I passed the school and saw a patch of new slates on the roof and an ugly iron barrier near the door to keep the homegoing children from rushing headlong on to the road. I knew if I had looked at the trees I'd have seen rusty drawing-pins stuck into their rough flesh. But I passed by. I heard there was a young teacher in the school now, with an array of coloured pencils in his breast pocket.

Michael McLaverty
The Game-cock and Other Stories

Michael McLaverty

A WEST CORK TALL TALE

'There was this man who was bringing a load on a cart from Cork to Macroom and it must have been a ton weight. And he saw that his horse, which was a jennet, was failing, but he really wanted to get to Macroom that night. Well, he had a bottle of poitín with him, and he put it back into the horse, and she was as lively as could be for another piece of the road. But just when he was to the East of Macroom, didn't the horse lie down on the road, under the load, and the divil the stir from her.

They thought that she was dead. There wasn't a move out of her, no matter what they did. One of the men with him said that they had as well make the best of it, and if they skinned her they could sell the skin in Macroom. So they set toe, and they skinned her, and when they had that done, she moved. She wasn't dead at all, only dead drunk on the poitín and the cold had put a stir into her when the skin was off.

They were in the divil of a fix, for the skin was after stiffening. One of them had an idea. There were sheep grazing in a field nearby, and they hopped over the wall and killed four of them and skinned them, and they sewed the warm skins on the horse, and she got up after her debauch, and pulled away as good as ever. Even after that he used to shear her twice a year — and you should have seen the grand fleece she had on her. She lived for fourteen years after that with two shearings a year.

Ah! the divil blast the lie is it? Wasn't I often talking to the son of the man who owned her!'

From *The Tailor and Ansty* by Eric Cross, but I was told the same story in Fermanagh in the North and Leitrim in the West.

CHAPTER 6 POITIN & COMMERCIAL WHISKEY

At the time of writing, if you go into an off license and purchase a bottle of 'Scotch' or 'Irish' you will probably have to pay approximately £4.40p. Of that, duty accounts for £3.16p, VAT 25p, marketing 58p. This leaves the cost of producing the bottle and its contents — 12p. That's right, 12 pence is all it costs to produce a bottle of nearly any proprietory brand of whisky (ey). The rest is tax and profit, and mainly tax at that, so, what exactly do you get for your money?

Firstly, it is important to distinguish between Malt and Grain Whisky. Malt whisky, traditionally made in Scotland, is made in pot stills, similar to those used to make Cognac, and is a unique blend of Malt, water and Scottish expertise and craftsmanship. You pay more for it, and, to the connoisseur, it is well worth it. The best Scottish Malt Whisky is the best in the world.

Opposed to that is Grain whisky, which accounts for 90% of the whisky market and includes all the well known brands such as Teachers, Haig, Johnny Walker, Black and White etc as well as what are now known as 'bargain' whiskies which appear and disappear in your local off license with startling regularity. This is a product of the industrial revolution and is manufactured on continuous process stills, similar to those used to make industrial alcohol and turpentine. It can be, and frequently is, made anywhere. A lot, it is true, is manufactured in the Lowlands of Scotland but as much again is manufactured in Bermondsey in London and other equally 'Sassenach' locations. All whiskies contain pentanol, because some malt at least is required to start the fermentation process in any whisky, but, because of an obscure court decision in 1909 a Royal Commission in that year ruled that grain whisky, although it only took three years to mature as opposed to a minimum of eight years for a malt whisky, was still entitled to describe itself as 'Scotch.' Nor did it have to disclose to the consumer the percentage — generally minute — of its product which is malt. The floodgates were opened.

Malt whisky, produced in the old fashioned pot still, is distinguished in taste and colour by the great amount of 'impurities' in it. That is what makes the genuine Highland malt whisky so good. Grain whisky on the other hand is colourless in its original state. Hence the use of a little malt to flavour it and caramel to colour it. Hence too the advertising to imply antiquity, for example 'Johnny Walker, born 1820 and still going strong.' This would be remarkable, since blended whiskies hadn't even been invented in 1820. What in fact it means is that DCL (Distillers Company Ltd), who control the lion share of the British whisky market, purchased a grocery business owned by a John Walker in Scotland who had founded his grocery shop in 1820 and sold whisky. It is interesting, although hardly surprising that DCL have always refused to divulge the contents of a bottle of their blended 'Scotch.' In the 1930s it has been estimated that the majority of proprietory brands of Scotch were at least 50% malt. Today the figure is nothing like that. The boom in Scotch sales has led to less and less malt being used and indeed last year the fastest growing whisky in the sales market, McArthurs, had so low a pentanol content as to suggest that it is 90% grain.

This is no concern of the customs or the chancellor however. They are not interested in quality control, only profit. Anyone who pays £15.75p for a license in Scotland and pays the excise the huge tax demanded is perfectly entitled to churn out the vilest rotgut, in bottles adorned with tartans, thistles and sporrans, and flog it to the unsuspecting and undiscerning public. And this brings us to poitin, for, as the reader will have gathered, the reason that the law says you cannot drink 'the mountain dew' has nothing whatsoever to do with the State's concern about your health; rather, it is the State's greed to get its hands on more and more revenue. Because the poitin maker is an independent soul, who resents giving the Government vast sums of money for doing nothing, he must be put down. And so the struggle goes on.

For whiskey is big business of course. For years it has been a major export. In 1976 over £436 million worth of Scotch was exported and the figures in the first half of 1977 show an increase of 22%. Of all the whisky(ey) made in Scotland and the North of Ireland (Bushmills and Coleraine) over 80% is sold overseas, mainly in the USA and Japan and the foreign currency this earns easily covers the imports of all foreign wines and spirits.

Poitin—the Genuine Article?

And compared to whiskey, what is poitin? This is difficult to answer. When I first started work on this book I believed that poitin could only be made from malt or barley. Anything else was but a pale imitation — bath-tub gin. Now I know that I was wrong. The word 'poitin' itself merely means 'a little pot.' In Ireland, through time it has come to mean a strong colourless spirit, not unlike whiskey in taste, which is illegally manufactured and upon which no duty is paid. In the 18th and 19th centuries it is true that barley, which was plentiful was generally used as the main ingredient, but even then there were dozens of different recipes and at times, when barley was scarce or expensive, substitutes were used. Today barley is in fact used by very few of the poitin makers I encountered. Each area has its own recipe involving malt or sugar or treacle or beet or potatoes depending on the market price and availability of whatever substance they prefer. The introduction of gas as an easy means of heating has changed the poitin makers modus operandi too, but, if care and attention is taken poitin made from just malt or beet or teacle or molasses can be every bit as good as that made from barley. Of course commercialism does exist. Tourists seeking Irish souvenirs are not infrequently sold rot gut and told that it's 'a drop of the quare stuff'. The only quare stuff likely to be in it is Parazone or Bluestone.

But this is nothing new. In the 18th century when in many areas every second house had its own still doubtless quality was universally high since most distillers would be their own best customers. But as the number of stills declined and the law interfered with a man's right to make himself a drink more and more people began to buy their dram from the local poitin maker rather than go to the trouble and risk of making it themselves. Complaints about 'bad bottles' grew. Obviously in a small isolated community where everyone knows everyone else the pressure is on the poitin maker to consistently come up with a high standard of poitin. Once transportation and communications open up the area and bring strangers there will be some who regard them as fair game. So it will always be. With poitin in particular the old maxim of 'Caveat emptor' is especially relevant. Some of the poitin I've sampled in the course of writing this book has been much smoother and more palatable than any parliament whiskey I've tasted. Some has been about the same and some has been downright rubbish. You pays yer money—and gets yourself a reliable supplier.

That brings me to the question of whether or not poitin should be legalised. In this section on Connemara the Comharchumann Cois Fharraige give their reasons why they think it should. In fact I disagree. Certainly it is iniquitous that the Government, any Government should tell anybody that they cannot manufacture a drink for themselves if they want to. All legislation against home brewing or distilling should be scrapped. Government's claims that such laws are for the good of people's health ring hollow when we see how much tax is raised from cigarettes and drink. Nor are governments too fastidious about quality control when it suits them, but when the Connemara co-op talk about legalizing poitin they are only really talking about legitimising themselves. If poitin making were permitted as a cottage industry in Connemara it would bring a few much needed jobs to the area, though I'm dubious about the figure of 1000 which Mr Lally quotes, but it would bring problems too. At present one of the main selling points of poitin is its price, around £2 a bottle. With no tax being paid this represents a very big profit for the manufacturer and a bargain for the consumer. If it were legalised a large amount of capital investment would be required since I can't see the big distillers allowing the Government to have a nationalised poitin industry. Poitin would obviously be taxed at the same rate as ordinary whiskey and with higher costs trying to break into the market could not sell at the same price. Most efforts would obviously be put into the export market. Local people couldn't afford to buy their own poitin, so what would they do? Out into the hills again and start making it illegally all over again. The greedy are sniffing around. The brand name 'Poitin' has been patented, but the 'cratur' has always thrived on illegality and there will, I hope, always be hardy souls who enjoy 'cheating' the exciseman.

Cartoon by Martyn Turner (*Irish Times*)

A Brief Note on Proof

The 'Proof' on a bottle frequently confuses people. This is hardly surprising. It is intended to. Before Mr Sikes, and Exciseman invented the hydrometer 'proof' was tested in a fairly cavalier fashion. A small heap of gunpowder was doused with a sample of the spirit which was being tested. A match was then put to the damp heap and if the result gave a steady flame the spirit was 'proved'. Too weak a mixture and the gunpowder only smouldered, too strong a one and you might get your silly head blown off. So much for 'quality control' in the good old days.

Since Sikes and his hydrometer however we now have more scientific definitions and tests. According to officialdom:-

'Spirits shall be deemed to be proof if the volume of the ethyl alcohol contained therein made up to the volume of the spirits with distilled water has a weight equal to that of 12/13ths of a volume of distilled water equal to the volume of spirits, the volume of each liquid being computed as at 51% Fa.'

In case you haven't quite grasped that, it means that 100° proof on the label means there's 57.06% alcohol in it if measured by volume or 48.24% alcohol if measured by weight. The British still use this ludicrous system of measurement but the Europeans and Americans use two different ones. By far the most sensible is the French system Gay-Lussac which simply expresses the proof figure in degrees, thus 40° on a French label means 40% alcohol. The Americans, who also have a smaller gallon, double this figure, thus 80° on a bottle of US Bourbon means it's 40% alcohol. The easiest way to convert British degrees-proof to percentage alcohol is to multiply by 4 and divide by 7. Thus the average bottle of spirits sold in British shops is marked 70° proof—or 40% pure alcohol.

Tourists drinking poitin. These intrepid British gentlemen must have astounded the natives, who probably gave them singlings, Co Clare, c 1890. (Welch Collection, Ulster Museum)

Cookstown, Co Tyrone, where according to a local doctor, 'the atmosphere was loaded with ether.' This photograph was taken at the turn of the century, when it is likely that the town was still 'an infected area.' (Green Collection, Ulster Folk Museum)

CHAPTER 7 BY-PRODUCTS OF POITIN

Poitin is a versatile spirit. A century ago some ingenious people came up with an unusual use for it. The practice had been common for years of selling off 'singlings', the first run, which is harsh, very strong and almost undrinkable, to people suffering from sprains, hacks and cuts. 'Just rub the singlings on and the pain will disappear like magic' it was widely believed. Singlings were also allowed to run until they would no longer ignite and then sold to farmers as cattle food. The cattle loved it and thrived on it. Indeed, in 1854 it was said that a man bringing a cow in peak condition to a Donegal fair was automatically suspected of illicit distillation, and the practice of feeding singlings to cattle continues to this day. But in the 1850s a new and strange use for singlings was discovered. In the Cookstown area of County Tyrone, a county where poitin was commonplace, poitin began to be sold to desperate or unscrupulous men who would add sulphuric acid to it. If put in a retort, the early distillate of this apparently appalling mixture was ether.

Ether drinking was strictly an Ulster phenomenon. To be even more precise, the 'infected area', as the Select Committee on British and Foreign Spirits of 1891 defined it, stretched from Pettigo in the West, up to Strabane, across to Dungiven and Kilrea, south to Toomebridge, down the Lough Shore to Portadown and then west again to Lisbellaw. Within this area, in the period 1850 — 1900 there were estimated to be a regular 50,000 'etheromaniacs', one in eight of the population of the area, annually consuming some 17,000 gallons of ether. Some local shebeens sold nothing else, in others, it stood side by side with poitin or even parliament whiskey on the shelf. Local chemists and grocers sold it by the pint and had plenty of customers. According to a local doctor 'the atmosphere of Cookstown and Moneymore was loaded with ether'; all around Draperstown a visiting surgeon detected 'the familiar smell'. The Times, in 1871 claimed that 'market days smelt not of pigs, tobacco smoke or unwashed human beings, but of ether.' Even the bank 'stoved' of ether while the smell of it on the Derry Central railway was 'disgusting and abominable.'

Ether is fairly vile stuff, so why was it so popular? Ken Connell, in his excellent essay on it described the ritual of drinking it thus — 'Ether volatizing at body temperature, tends to escape as a gas on contact with mouth or stomach, and, irritating the stomach, it is likely to be ejected by vomiting. But a ritual was evolved enabling the drinker to retain enough of so elusive a beverage to experience its gratifying effect. After renching his gums (rinsing out the mouth with cold water) a man would drink a little water, hold his nose, and quickly swallow the ether, following it down with more water. The water lessened the burning effect, the nose holding lessened the risk of vomiting.'

Dosage, it seems, varied. Young girls were advised not to take more than a teaspoonful, while hardened male 'etheromaniacs' could swallow an egg cup full.

Up to half a pint a day might be consumed this way — or a pint on a fair day debauch. For beginners it was, hardly surprisingly, very unpleasant at first, the eyes watered, the stomach burned and you were exceedingly likely to throw up; but what if you managed to persevere, what delights awaited one?

According to the Times reporter, who seems to have got rather more interested in ether than professional dispassionateness would normally permit, 'after a few minutes one's pulse quickened, the face flushed, one became calm and detached and dreamed oneself in paradise.' Cares vanished in 'blithesome gladness, eyes glistened with love, you heard music everywhere.' You also hallucinated quite a bit it appears. A County Tyrone account claimed that 'frequently you saw men climbing up the walls and going through the roof.' Some trip eh! Lascivious continentals who were also for a time very fond of ether — you could even get it in pastille form like wine gums — claimed that it acted like an aphrodisiac, but the steadier and more rational Paddy and his wife had no time for such erotic nonsense. They just saw little men climbing up walls.

This 'trip' lasted only about twenty minutes. The imbiber would then return to reality, sober and without a hangover. Thus a man or woman could be drunk half a dozen times a day without having either a hangover or empty pockets, for the cost, about a penny a tablespoonful, meant that for threepence a drinker could have, as the Times put it, 'a blissful fair day.' It was alleged that ether drinking was 'a Romanish vice', and some even claimed that you could 'tell a man's religion by smelling his breath' — shades of a certain political reactionary cleric of today—but in fact this was not really true. Many a good 'loyal' Protestant and his wife in 'the infected area' was fond of a drop of the 'aythur' . It was the Catholic Church however which first tried to put a stop to this practice. In 1869 ether drinking was 'cursed by the priest of Maghera', to little or no effect apparently, since in 1889 we hear of the Rev. Edward Callen, Catholic curate of Granahan and Maghera still having to proscribe it to his flock. Later, he and his fellow clerics went so far as to buy up the entire stock of ether in Draperstown and sell it back, allegedly at a loss, to the supplier, in a vain attempt to deny the etheromaniacs their tipple, and soon ether drinking was made a reserved sin.

Ether drinking seems to have originated in the Draperstown area some time around the 1840s, when an unemployed and alcoholic doctor, who had tried it himself, induced some neighbours to follow his example, claiming that it was 'a preventative for cholera and like diseases'. It is, of course, no such thing, but debate was to rage in the columns of The Lancet no less, as to the beneficial or harmful properties of ether. Despite the horror tales that circulated about ether, usually emanating from a clerical or temperance source, according to The Lancet of 1890 'ether is not very addictive and is a relatively benign poison compared with alcohol. Organic diseases caused by its habitual consumption are small compared with the ravages alcohol leaves in its train'. So it seems that the stories of etheromaniacs in their early forties being 'wizened, beat, decrepit tottering old men, battered and lonely hulks cast up on the shores of existence, hopeless and despairing human wrecks' as one cleric put it, are, to say the least, exaggerated.

There was one very real danger however associated with ether drinking, fire. The ether would 'kill or bust you if you didn't rift' (belch) immediately after swallowing as explosive volatization could constrict the heart. 'Rifting' wasn't too hard to do, but if, under the influence, one forgot and rifted near a fire the resulting flames, caused by the ether vapour mixing with the air, could travel down your throat. Connell quotes a Bellaghy farmer who witnessed a friend lighting his pipe and igniting his breath. 'The fire cot his breath, and tuk fire inside, and only for a man that was carryin' a jug of wathur wud some poitin to the kitchen he'd have lost his life. We just held him down at wanst, as quick as we cud, and poured the wather down his throat.' It's a good job they didn't pour the poitin down instead! Drinkers were sometimes brought to Cookstown workhouse almost burnt to death by ether and a Draperstown poor law guardian told an inquiry in 1891 of an explosion of ether in a local shop which killed four people.

Still, although it could be lethal, as the popularity of poitin declined in the area due to the temperance campaigns of the churches, ether continued to be drunk, and it was not the churches who finally stamped out the practice but the law. (Indeed during Father Theobald Matthew's temperance campaign in the 1840s and 50s many signed the pledge and forsook poitin and parliament whiskey but upped their consumption of ether — 'sure it wasn't the same as alcohol.')

In 1890 ether was scheduled under the Poisons Act of 1870 and the legal sale of it dropped dramatically overnight. Blackmarket ether or the home made poitin/sulphuric brand were still available, but at an inflated price. The practice lingered on however and in 1923 the Northern Ireland Minister for Home Affairs conceded that 'in some areas it is widely used.' The 1927 Intoxicating Liquor and Licensing Act (NI) more or less finally put an end to this somewhat bizarre drinking habit. Winos could still drink or inhale meths or 'pennydrunk' (coal gas bubbled through milk) or mix boot polish with hot water and filter it through bread, but an era was over. Licensed distilling, with Government assistance had won. Only the humble poitin maker continues, somewhere out in the mists.

Donegal peasants of the type described by MacGowan. The Victorian cameraman was probably Robert French. (Lawrence Collection, National Library of Ireland)

CHAPTER 8 THE OLD CRAFT CONTINUES

When Gardai entered a dwelling house they found 30 gallons of 'wash' simmering in a barrel under the heat of an electric blanket, Justice McGahon was told in Crossmolina Court, Co. Mayo, yesterday.

Geoffrey Fair, Erris Street, Crossmolina, was charged with eight offences in connection with illicit distillation. He was fined £100 on each of two charges of having a pint of poteen and a still. The other charges were struck out.

A charge against Seamus Dolan, Enniscoe, Crossmolina, of being in a place where illicit distillation was in progress was dismissed.

Supt. Daniel Kennedy said that on December 12 Sgt. Sharkey and Garda Dunlea searched the defendant's house and found a quantity of poteen in bottles.

In an upstairs room they found 30 gallons of wash in a wooden barrel which was covered by an electric blanket which was switched on.

The wash was in an advanced stage of fermentation and was simmering under the heat. Fair explained that the barrel was used for salting a pig which he had killed.

When they searched the upstairs portion of the premises they found Dolan, fully clothed, in bed and he appeared to be suffering from a bad hangover.

Sgt. Sharkey said the place was littered with bottles and his attention was drawn to the electric blanket by a pilot light.

Irish Press

There are still some who can recall making poitin in the 1920s and 30s. Willie McKeever, now 74, from Crosskey near Ahoghill is one such man. He and his neighbours made 'wee still', as poitin is called locally, for almost half a century. He can remember when the use of the old fashioned worm began to die out, to be replaced by the more modern condenser. 'There were different kinds of worms,' he recollects, 'I well remember seeing a chair worm that looked like this $\bigwedge\bigwedge\bigwedge\bigwedge$, with about six inches to every joint up in a neighbours loft in 1920. By then condensers were all the rage. We used to make them out of the bodies of three old knapsack sprayers if we couldn't get a tinker to make one. This kind of still didn't last that long you know. It would get tarnished and affect the taste and you'd have to get another one. In those days most of the local farmers were making wee still, but everyone was wild cautious. They all feared getting gripped.' (by the RUC). 'I was niver gripped meself, but was damn near twice. Once me and some others were up on the moss (turf bog) making wee still. There was this big blacksmith who had come up to watch. We used to keep the barrels down under the moss. This would be about 1930. Well, nothing would do this big fellow but that he'd have to try some of the gyle (wash) to drink and, sure enough he collapsed and two of the boys had to carry him back home through the fog. That left two of us and there we were, in the middle of the night, up on the moss with the still going strong when I smelt the rubber of their coats. I can niver forget that smell. Two big RUC men, and I sees this big hand coming round the corner of the ditch. But I'd smelt their coats first and we tuk off, jumping the bogs and the ditches. We lost the still and about four gallons of wee still but they niver catched us. We found out later that they had been watching that spot for three days after following a trail of turf that had dropped out of a wee hole in a bag we'd brought up the last time we'd used that place. We allus cleaned up after a night on the moss and buried the barrels but we must have missed this.

We used to make lovely wee still. 10 stone of treacle, 3½ pounds of yeast would give you 4 or 4½ gallons. Demarara sugar was good too if you could get it. The wee still used to sell for about 12/- a pint but you'd need to be careful who you sold it to — and who you bought the treacle from. There were men gripped because the grocer informed on anyone buying a large amount of treacle or sugar. You would get three or six months if you were gripped. To anyone making it, I'd just say, when there's cobwebs round the whiskey, its time she's off and when you're doubling it (second run) keep the heat down for she's thick as your finger.'

After this mysterious advice, it's only fair to say that in the Ahoghill area now people don't have to spend any more cold and dangerous nights up on the moss. Condensers have cut half a night's work down to two hours and the advent of gas has meant that one can make wee still indoors now. And a last word to Willie McKeever, 'For nine years I made gallons of wee still sitting in one wee room, day in, day out. I'll not say how long ago that was either. And divil a bit of harm did it do me or anyone I gave it to!'

County Antrim

County Antrim has always been poitin country. Ever since the plantation when the settlers moved in and forced the indigenous Catholic population off the farm lands and up into the hills illicit distillation has been going on. Life up the Glens was hard. The land was poor and little would grow yet rents had to be paid and so poitin making was an obvious trade for some. Until the building of the Antrim coast road the area was remote and a distiller perched at the head of the glen could spot a policeman or revenue man coming for miles. The water was clear, the skills were there and the trade flourished. At the times of the old 'Stanin dram' public houses — so called because the customer bought his drink and had to stand outside by the road to drink it — poitin or 'wee still' was commonly sold.

As in the rest of Ireland the trade declined by the 20th century, but the glens have retained a reputation for poitin to this day. Partly this was due to Mickey McIlhatten, 'the King of the Glens', certainly the best known and respected poitin maker in the county for many years, but he was by no means the only illicit distiller nor even the best. There was McGoldrick from Rasharkin whose skill was such that he was offered a small fortune to go to America during Prohibition to teach bootleggers but refused. Some of his poitin was matured in sherry casks and turned constantly on chains to produce what some locals have described as 'nectar'. (In the Appalachians kegs were attached to the grandmother's rocking chair.)

Then there was the proud poitin maker from Glenwhery, a great cock fighting area, who was so proud of his produce and his reputation that he used to label every bottle with his own label — Moore's Melody. And there was Cunningham from Cushendun direction who was raided by the police. They searched high and low and were about to give up when an irascible Sergeant spied a large number

*The King of the Glens, the late Mick
McIlhatten. (Crosskeys Inn)*

of empty treacle tins. 'You're caught now', he shouted, 'what else would you be doing with all that treacle but making poitin'.

'Sure, I can't stand jam' was the reply.

Most of the stories of poitin making in Antrim are, of course, about McIlhatten, the King. A shepherd, life long Republican — he was interned on the Argenta and imprisoned without trial in Larne Workhouse in 1920 — traditional musician, gentleman and poitin maker par excellence. McIlhatten made poitin for over fifty years, and had several recipes, one of which included adding crushed apples to the mash to add potency. Despite his fame he was rarely caught, and this was because he was so well respected. Even some of the local Orange men would come to him before the annual Twelfth processions and surreptitiously purchase half a dozen or so bottles to keep up their spirits. During the second world war, when spirits were hard to get, many a supposedly 'respectable' citizen, including judges and doctors, would approach him for 'a cure' and generally he was able to oblige. Similarly, a certain, now prominent Unionist politician and some Army officers on occasion joined him on one of his frequent poaching expeditions. Thus established as a 'character' the King had few enemies and many friends. His first conviction was only a small fine after he had solemnly assured the Resident Magistrate that 'a man from Sligo had told me that a rub of poitin on a fiddle makes it sound all the sweeter.' The police knew all about him but regarded him as no trouble. Besides, some of them liked a drop also, hence there was stunned shock when in 1967, in his late sixties he was apprehended by a zealous young copper and hauled before the petty sessions court at Cloughmills. He had been away playing the fiddle up country and so hadn't got the warning tip off and a cask of poitin was found in his turf stack — luckily, as he was later to say, they didn't find the large cache concealed nearby. His title as 'king' dates from then as his lawyer, in an impassioned plea in his defence, told the RM that it was almost lese-majestie to try a king on such a charge. The newspapers took the story up and the title stuck but Mickey was sent to the Crumlin Road jail for four months. In the event he didn't have to serve all his sentence for when various members of the bar, who had all sampled his wares at one time or another, heard about it a whip round paid off the remaining part of his fine. (He had been offered a fine stead of imprisonment but scornfully turned down such a bargain). But he never forgot the young policeman whose zealousness had put him behind bars. He always referred to the officer, a small burly man, not by name, but as 'my little friend' and years later when he went over to England to appear on the Dave Allen TV programme he was still careful to seek legal advice about what his 'little friend' might do if he was to bring a bottle of poitin over to the 'Sassanachs.'

The King, alas, is dead, but in County Antrim today some still follow his trade. As recently as July 1977 the Ballymena Observer had headlines about Ballymena publicans bewailing the increasing poitin market which was, they claimed, hitting their profits. Visions of impoverished publicans queuing at the dole were conjured up as they spoke angrily of poitin being widely available in the streets of Ballymena for £2 a pint. Six independent producers were alleged to have the trade sewn up and Portglenone, Cullybackey, Cargan, Broughshane and Ballymena itself were all mentioned as production centres. Their claims may be slightly hysterical — and, in some cases hypocritical as some publicans have not been above buying poitin themselves and cutting it with parliament whiskey to sell to unsuspecting customers — but it is true that poitin manufacture in the area is on the increase. In the North Antrim area the last prosecution for illicit distillation was in 1973 and the offending party only got a £15 fine. Potatoes, treacle and yeast are easily available, the police have other things on their minds, and there seems no reason to suppose that the people of the area will lose the taste for 'wee still' that many of them have acquired.

Note: County Antrim was the scene, in 1965, of two deaths attributed to poitin. This has led to the kind of hysterical generalization that is frequently made by the popular press that 'if you drink poitin you'll go blind or die or both.' This ludicrous assertion has the same validity as scare stories about smoking marihuana and going insane or taking LSD and immediately jumping out of a tenth storey window under the impression that you're a golden eagle. The truth about the Broughshane deaths was that two idiots decided to make some 'stuff' for themselves and used a barrel that had contained weedkiller to brew in without even washing it out. It was weedkiller and stupidity that killed them, not poitin. This is not to say of course that if you buy a bottle allegedly containing poitin from a complete stranger you mightn't end up with something rather vile which would do your health no good at all.

A Visit to West Cork

In the past County Cork was not noted as one of the main poitin producing areas. In the 19th century it didn't figure in the 'Top Ten'. Things have changed however. Within a small area of West Cork and County Kerry there are upward of a hundred stills in regular use, each turning out its own special recipe for 'Katie Daly' as they call it.

The first thing the visitor notices is the incredible hospitality offered by the people to strangers. In the half dozen or so houses we were in during an all too brief visit the kettle was automatically put on the stove as soon as we entered. No one dreamed of offering us tea, 'a glass of punch' was always offered. The well known song 'The Jug of Punch' comes from this area and almost every household seems to drink it. The kettle is boiled, the glass or mug heated, hot water poured in, sugar added and then the lemonade bottle full of poitin is produced. Large steaming glasses of poitin punch are passed around and 'the crack' begins.

For instance, they might tell you of Jer Sean Jer, 'now 99 or 101, no one can remember', who was stopped on his motor bike in 1921 by the Black and Tans. 'Where the hell did you get the petrol for that wreck you Irish bastard!' they shouted. Jer Sean drew himself up to his full height and answered in as dignified a manner as possible, 'Yerra, sure 'tis poitin driving the bike and 'tis poitin driving the man.' He was telling the truth too, and on returning home he used to siphon out a wee drop for a nightcap. Shell oil beware!

The visitor to the area, if privileged, might get a trip to the infamous 'Smokey Tavern', an old farm house, up in the hills. Approaching it after a meandering drive through low hills, along boreens and through people's back yards the visitor is greeted by the owner 'Paddy Muldoon' who issues you in and regales you with extremely tall tales about his prowess with a gun while serving you the while with hot fiery punch. His eight dogs and six cats help give the 'Smokey Tavern', with its soot blackened walls, its own distinctive aroma and encourage the weak stomached to have another large mug of 'the good stuff'. Muldoon (not his real name), mug in hand, turns to a matter that has vexed him for years. The guards. His feud with them is long standing. One guard in particular he hates. 'Three times I had the bastard in the sights of my gun and three times I didn't pull the trigger', he moans. 'An then, only the next week sure didn't he arrest me in the town for making a wee drop of the stuff. I niver told him how lucky he was.' Personally, having seen the ancient Boer War rifle involved and Muldoon's shaking hands, I think the Gardai had little to worry about, but, I could always be wrong. Muldoon's uncle, then aged 86, won the unofficial area rifle shooting competition up the mountain last year displaying astonishing marksmanship despite a lifetime of 'sitting with Katie Daly'.

Muldoon settles down, mug of punch in hand, to tell you of 'the good old days' when he made the 'cratur' — terriers we called it. You'd go up to this boyo in the bar and ask him if he wanted a couple of terriers. Sometimes he didn't, but, more often, he did. You'd wander up the road a bit, reach into the ditch and give him the bottles. He'd give you a few shillings (current price £2 a bottle) and back you'd go into the bar. It was all made from barley and malt in them days. Usually in quantities of about 40 gallons at a time though of course, there's a few make it in bigger quantities now. The turf gave it a lovely smokey flavour. That's how this house got its name, of course. I used to have it going all the time here. Now I leave it to the younger men, (he lies unconvincingly). I could still teach them a thing or two about it but. Nowadays they use sugar or treacle without the barley to save themselves trouble. It may taste all right, but it's not the same. Now this', he says, suddenly brandishing an apparently inoffensive Lucozade bottle he's produced out of nowhere, 'now this is the real thing. It'll knock yer feckin head off.' It nearly did, but the faithful Igor and I awoke in our beds the next morning with not a trace of a hangover or upset stomach, just hazy memories of a night in 'the Smokey Tavern.'

Modern poitin-making, somewhere in West Cork, 1976. This series of pictures courtesy of the Cork Examiner, shows something of the primitive surroundings where the 'cratur' is made.

1 Primitive surroundings, but fairly typical for today's rural poitin-maker.

2 *Support home industries! Only Irish sugar used.*

3 The worm is simple, but effective enough.

4 A simple heat source.

5 The singlings appear. These would have to be run through again to make a reasonable drink.

Once poitin was everywhere in County Donegal. The County was, according to Government reports, 'notorious'. To the people it was as natural to have a still house as to have a cow. Stories of poitin and references to it are commonplace in memoirs of the county in the last century. What follows are a few extracts from different sources which show how 'the little pot' was taken for granted. The first comes from the Irish 'Rotha Mór an tSaoil', translated as 'The Hard Road to Klondike'. The speaker is the late Micky MacGowan who lived in Magheraoarty, near Gortahork in the 1860s and 1870s.

'My own people were making poitin just the same as everyone else. Not to put a tooth in it, they were somewhat astray because of it. They had neither a day's peace or a night's rest on account of it and it sent enough of them such a way that they hardly knew what they were doing. At times they would drink so much of it that they'd go off their heads altogether ... There weren't many to keep an eye on the poitin makers in those days other than the crowd we used to call the 'Watermen'. (Water-bailiffs) ... Near enough to the houses the poitin was made. There wasn't a rivulet or stream in the place that hadn't a still-house beside it. A good sized stream with the best of water in it flows down between our house and Magheraoarty. Down by the main road there's a sizeable fall in the stream and, at the foot of this fall, my own people had a fine still-house. There's a nice secluded little dell in that place and, if you didn't know it was there, you'd never find it.'

MacGowan went on to describe a chase by the Watermen in which an innocent bystander was run through with a bayonet and killed when one of the Watermen panicked. Poitin has had other martyrs in the County too. In Teelin, in South-West Donegal a lament is still sung about Shane O'Haughey who died in the cause of the 'great white spirit.' The first verse goes:-

Sheághain, a rúin, is tú bhí tapaidh in do láimh,
Agus le barr do mhéir go ngléasthá culaidh ar bhád;
Na tonna bhí tréan ag éirghe tharat go h-árd,
'S a charaid mo chléibh, níor fhéad tú imtheacht ó'n bhás.

(Dearest Sean, you had the skilled hands and could dress a boat with the tips of your fingers. The waves towering above you were powerful, and, dear friend, you could not escape death).

What it doesn't say was that Sean's skilled fingers were also used to make poitin and that he and two companions were drowned off Aughris Head on the Sligo coast in 1803 because the barley they were carrying in the small boat became waterlogged. Sean who was steering and the others had an argument as to whether the poitin barley should be sacrificed and agreed to start throwing it overboard but in doing so capsized the boat and drowned. A tragic tale.

Another tragic, although perhaps a little implausible story comes from the Finntown Gaeltacht in mid-Donegal. It comes from a collection of folk tales by Seaghan MacMeanman published by the Gaelic League.

'When we reached my house in Finntown we discovered that some of the neighbourhood women had gathered there before us, and they were absolutley delighted to learn that I had a Spanish doctor with me instead of an old midwife. The doctor hadn't been there long until twins were born, a boy and a girl. The doctor wouldn't wait to eat or drink anything but went off in a great hurry. The poitin was plentiful; the women were talking and arguing and debating about this and that; so it wasn't until sunrise that anyone noticed that the little boy had been abducted and that a big-pawed, club-footed changeling with the face of an old man had been left in his place! Ah! Then I knew that the doctor had been a fairy.' In the throes of the poitín Manus had obviously forgotten to make an offering of the first (and best) drop of the poitín to 'Red Willy', the Donegal fairy who had the power over the excisemen and other local bad spirits.

The same Manus was a great man for the poitín, much to his wife's disgust, for she used to lock him up in the house as much as possible lest 'if he got out without someone to keep an eye on him, straight-away he'd make for one of the little poitín distilling huts that are situated here and there along both banks of the river Finn. The poitín distillers would give him plenty to drink, and poor man, he wouldn't know when he had had his fill.' Manus was in his element at weddings and wakes however, and there are many descriptions in the stories of feasts, with men, women, boys and girls coming from all over the area. 'There was always a big turf fire and another in the kitchen that would roast a boar. There was venison (poached of course), fish, potatoes, wheaten bread and lashings of poitín. The priest himself would be sitting in the corner telling stories about the time he was in Paris, which is in France, and the teacher would be telling tales about the time he was in Derry and the wonders he had seen there. Seamus Mankin would be playing the pipes and the boys and girls would be dancing. After midnight Michael Murray and Felim McFadden would slip out to the wee still house for the reserve supply of poitín that had been left there the previous day for fear the Surveillance people (Inland Revenue) from Dungloe might come that way. . . .'

The Donegal Novelist Seamas MacGrianna, who died recently, was born in Ranafast, Co Donegal in 1891. He wrote in Irish under the pseudonym 'Maire' and has left in his autobiography Nuair a bhí mé óg ('When I was Young'), the following account of poitín:

'My father was a marvellous storyteller. Many a time we sat round the fire on a long winter's night without a word, listening to him, and few nights went by without a couple of stories about the people who made poitín and the Revenue men. . . . When my father was a boy there was an Inland Revenue barracks in the town of Glenties and the man in charge was a fellow called Costello. Many a time Costello and his squad of men would take our town-land in the rear in a search for poitín. Six of them would usually arrive, all on horseback. You wouldn't have time to take two glances at them from the time they would suddenly appear on the shoulder of Deeragh Hill till they would be at the top of Caracaman. Sometimes they would come and lift lots of booty, at other times the men of our area would be too quick for them and they had to leave empty handed. The latter were the best Revenue stories my father told. When the encounters were won by the Revenue men my father hadn't half the zest in telling the tale nor we in listening to it, but when the men from the Rosses proved stronger than the Queen's men, I'm telling you we heard a story worth hearing.

Many a time it seemed to me that I was watching them with my mind's eye: Black Paddy escaping from six of them in broad daylight and he carrying a still on his back: or Big Owen Neill's ''mad mare'' coming into Losset bog on a fine summer's evening. Owen on her back and two kegs of poitín in front of him. Costello and his posse in hot pursuit, the leading rider coming within two lengths of him at Meenadreen bends. ''Mad mare'' getting her wind back on the height above Lough Aginnive and coming down Dunlewy brae like the March wind. Owen looking over his shoulder at Meenacung to discover no sign of life or limb within eyeshot or earshot.'

These stories had a profound effect on young Seamas. Not for him and his friends childish games of Cowboys and Indians, no, they played Poitin men and Revenuemen.

'Johnny was Costello and I was Manny, the best poitin maker in the three parishes. I well remember the first "warming" we did. We had a fire in a rock-cleft in Portacurry and a bucket, a couple of small mugs and an old can. Well, at least that's what the uninitiated would have seen but to us, we had every conceivable piece of apparatus that an expert distiller would have had. A head, a worm, a still, barrels, vats, malt, yeast and fermented worts. Hudai Hugh was helping me with the run. My brother Donal and Johnny Hugh were in the Revenue and were spying on us from the back of Gubnabansha. Both of them had a donkey by the halter and both were ready to mount and gallop across the sandbank at top speed just when Hudai and I would have the barrels "warmed". But we had our dog Bran there with us as well and he was a good guard dog.

We started distilling and it wasn't long until she was coming round. I caught a drop of the "poitin" in a limpet shell and we both took a sip of it and declared that it was as fine a drop as was ever made. We were working away and footering about and conversing like a pair of old men. "Smother that fire a wee bit Hudai," says I, "you've too much heat at the still."

"Is she coming down pale?" asks Hudai.

"She's not as clear as I'd like" says I. Just with that Bran let a yelp out of him that echoed along the cliffs. Up the rocks went Hudai like the March wind. He was no sooner up than he was pelting down.

"Oh by my soul and our God, Manny, aren't Costello and his men on top of us! Take you the worm!" And he snatched the still from the fire and the race began.

Out on to the strand we went, and all the equipment with us. When we were at Lecknalua Costello's mounted horde appeared at Gobnasligan. Out on to the big sandbank we raced with the cans and the bucket making a terrible racket and Bran at our heels with the yowls of him being heard for miles.'

Alas, in Donegal those days are long past. The children now would be more likely to be playing Kojak. Some poitin is still made in the County of course, but mainly for the tourists and usually of poor quality. The days of Inishowen's dominance are gone. Around Ranafast or Teelin you might get a drop and elsewhere in the County the odd rounds-man might still deliver a bottle or two with the milk or the groceries but the days when poitin was the king are no more here.

In the County Clare

Although Clare is mentioned quite a bit in the old songs about poitin, it was never one of the great distilling counties and probably owes its reputation more to the fact that more words rhyme with Clare than do with Connemara. Poitin is still made there of course, but no longer in great quantity. Old 'Pa' who has been making it for 24 years bemoans the changes that have taken place during that time.

'Some of the blackguards that are making it now don't care about making a decent drop. It's just the quick shilling they're after. They use the Bluestone (a kind of insecticide) or washing soda to clear the stuff. It looks clear and it's quick but the stuff's poisonous. You can always tell it's bad by the way a drop of it will curdle milk. The commercialism around here is killing the trade. That and the Guards. These days some of them never give a man peace. I've never used anything artificial in my stuff, just barley, yeast and water. In the past people would have come miles for my tusabhocta — the first sip of the first run.'

Visitors to various well known coastal villages in Clare over the past few years may well have brought back a bottle of 'the stuff,' which, they were solemnly assured was 'made on the islands' . It is most unlikely that it was. 'Pa ', who operated quite a few miles inland used to sell his product to local entrepreneurs who would water it down, jack up the price, and sell to the unwary tourist. A few years ago the guards did make a haul of poitin equipment and wash on Inisheer, but since then the islands off Clare have been reported quiet — although I hope someone will prove me wrong on this.

Poitin in the Lurgan Area

There is no tradition of poitin making in the North Armagh area along the shores of Lough Neagh. Any that was available usually came from the mountains of Pomeroy in County Tyrone and the last time that it was at all plentiful in the Lurgan - Portadown region was in the early and mid sixties when the labourers who constructed that section of the M1 motorway came from East Tyrone. There was, however, one exception, and this was at Annaghdroghal, in the 1920's and 30's. Annaghdroghal is in fact in County Down. It is a tiny strip of land, in part only a thousand yards in width which squeezes its way between Counties Armagh and Antrim to the shore of Lough Neagh. Because of this freak in the drawing of the boundary the area came under the jurisdiction of the County Down constabulary and not the nearby Lurgan RUC. In those days police boundaries were regarded as almost sacrosanct by the different

stations and so the local family who made poitin for well over a decade felt fairly safe; if the worst came to the worst they used to shift the equipment a few hundred yards across the County Armagh border. They wouldn't be so lucky today.

A MODERN BELFAST RECIPE

Whether this can technically be called poitin is a moot point, but that's what the manufacturer, operating in an old garage somewhere in Belfast calls it and, when properly made it doesn't taste too bad.

At least four stone of oranges.
8 pounds of sugar (brown).
1½ ozs yeast.
10 gallons of water.
Carrots can be added if you want to take away the Orange flavour, in which case there will be a gin-like taste.

The oranges are peeled and put in a plastic bin. Then, an exotic touch, they are trampled to a mush by a barefoot lady (who doesn't *have* to be a virgin, but it might help). The mush is left for three to four weeks or until you can't stand the smell any more or the neighbours complain. A milk churn and an improvised worm made out of copper is then used to distil this rather revolting mixture. This produces a drink with a message, and the message is *Beware!*

Another intrepid experimeter in Belfast is producing an explosive brew by distilling nettle wine. He makes the wine in the usual way, lets it mature for a few months and then distills the stuff, using an ordinary Liebig condenser and with a charcoal filter on the first run. After being run through three times the end product is so strong that it has to be watered down at least twice. It tastes not unlike second grade West Cork poitin.

Modern urban still, somewhere in Belfast 1977. Uses a Burco boiler; pipes lead to kitchen sink; leibig condenser in tube. Latest recipe, 7lbs malt, 6lbs sugar for every 5 gallons.

'Keep your eyes well peeled today, the tall tall men are on their way, searching for the mountain tae, in the hills of Connemara.'

Connemara and Galway are still two of poitin's strongholds. The troubles in the North have hit poitin making in the border areas like Cavan and Monaghan although the transfer of more gardai to these areas has conversely helped the moonshiners of Sligo and Leitrim, but it is in the rugged terrain around Ballinakill or Lettermore or Inverin that you see the old crafts flourishing. Christmas is the high-point of the year for poitin manufacturers and salesmen in these parts — much of the merchandise is brought all over the country and to England and America by holidaying exiles — and it is during the months leading up to the festivities that a strange ritual takes place.

This is 'the swoop'. Led by a larger than life figure Superintendent Patrick Gallagher 'veteran of a thousand swoops' and his faithful sidekick 'the shrewd-faced Garda Michael Dowd' the poitin squad leave their HQ in Oughterard and descend upon the countryside to 'put the fear of God into the poitin makers.' So, at least, the newspapers would have us believe. Every year readers of the national press are treated to such flights of ungrammatical literary fancy as 'Dowd is a quiet spoken Kerryman, with slow, mellow Gaelic and a ruddy face which above its blue serge and shining buttons is the most dreaded manifestation of the law in Connacht's poteen country.' Or how about 'Supt. Gallagher, known locally as the Hammer, spoke slowly and calmly. 'Another good week boys, 2 forty gallon barrels, 440 gallons of wash, two stills, two worms. We are containing them. We are hitting them hard. We are driving them to the water's edge!'

According to this version of the state of play in Connemara, the very mention of 'Dowd from Dingle' or 'the Hammer' causes strong men to clench their teeth, women to wring their hands and children to burst into tears. The myth is backed up by headlines such as 'Poitin drought expected this Year', 'Commando style raids on the poitin makers', 'Biggest haul ever, £8,000 worth of poitin seized.' The last story goes on to relate a thrilling tale, of how, under the inspiring leadership of 'the Hammer' a six man squad 'swooped' (what else?) on a remote mill lake at Ballinakill.

'A brown sheepdog at the lakeshore barked a warning as Garda Gaughan led Sgt. O'Riordan and Sgt. McCole on a sharp sprint from the road to the lake shore. Warned by the dog however, two men shot away across the lake in a rowboat and escaped while almost simultaneously another pair of moonshiners evaded Gardai O'Connor and Cosgrove and made their lightning getaway over the water. The haul was a huge one however. The first stillhouse, cleverly concealed by stone walls right on the lakeshore had not one but two stills in it. The wash was still red hot and steaming in three barrels, the gas was buring and the worm still dripping prime poitin into a white enamel bucket. As they smashed up the equipment and razed the stonehouses to the ground the feared Garda Dowd said 'This must be the thirtieth time or so I've been on a raid to this lake.'

'There'll be drunk fishes tonight' quipped Sgt. O'Riordan as he poured the beer, like a yellow river, into the lake, while Garda Cosgrove, a well known Galway footballer, opened the valves on the gas cylinders and sent them speeding torpedo-like across the lake.'

With 'the Hammer' on a raid at a lake, near Ballinakill, Connemara. (Photographs by Colman Doyle)
1 Right beside the lake, the poitín squad come upon the stillhouse, concealed by stone walls.

2 The haul's a good one!

3 The Wash is still hot.

4 *The equipment is dismantled and the gas cylinders are 'torpedoed' away.*

5 But, warned of the Garda's approach by a sheepdog, the poitin-makers escape in a rowboat across the lake.

Stirring stuff! The media loves it. In addition to all the coverage in the Irish Press, Independent and Times the TV men get in on the act. NBC, ITV, and BBC have all recently done mock humourous pieces on poitin including Bernard Falk's ludicrously staged raid for Nationwide. RTE frequently do features about it and a new 16 mm film, called amazingly enough, 'Poteen' and starring Cyril Cusack, Niall Tobin, Donal McCann and 'a host of local actors' is being shot on location near Carraroe by Bob Quinn. But how accurate is the picture the media generally report? Is it really about stern faced Guards relentlessly doing their duty and smashing stills while nimble footed moonshiners make good their escape by land or water? Of course not. Occasionally we get a 'humourous' story, such as the raid near Inverin when the 'moonshiners' recaptured their confiscated poitin which had been locked up in the police station, but mostly it is a routine business. The poitin maker tries to continue to make his product and sell it without being too conspicuous and the Guards try to make sufficient siezures a year to justify their existence but not so many that they would make themselves redundant. The old old story.

In 1977 a new angle was added however. The Comharchumann Cois Fharraige, a Connemara based co-op whose Public Relations Officer is the vociferous Michael Lally began its campaign to have poitin making legalized and established locally as a craft industry. How the press loved that. TV crews even came from the continent to film. 'The Gardai captured £63,000 worth of poitin and equipment in this area in 1976,' says Lally. 'This represents only about 12% of the total amount of poitin manufactured during the peak season September to Christmas. At least 60 men are making it full time here in Connemara, turning out some £750,000 worth a year. In addition there are at least 40 other non-commercial manufacturers. One big operator has a £50,000 turnover. Based on a market survey we reckon that, properly controlled for quality an internationally marketed poitin could bring in annually £12-£15 million pounds and employ up to 1,000 people.'

Mr Lally's enthusiasm is infectious although his figures have been known to fluctuate according to which newspaper you read, but, whether or not the figure of £12 million can stand up (at times it is projected as £20 million within the next decade) there is no doubt that on a local level at least poitin making can still be very profitable. For every £30.80p spent on barley, sugar and yeast the Connemara poitin maker reckons to get back £400. The trade name 'Poitin' has been already patented and the campaign for legalization will continue in Connemara no doubt. Elsewhere I've given my reasons for not being in favour of legalization but at least the campaign shows that poitin making in the West is still in a healthy state, despite 'The Hammer' and 'Dowd from Dingle'. And this brings me to the point. It has become a ritual, a pantomine. The Gardai get publicity and a few rewards for their seizures, the press get their stories and the poitin maker, taking advantage of the publicity can up his price and his profits — in the last five years or so the price of a pint bottle of 'the stuff' in Connemara has almost doubled. In some places the unsuspecting could even have to fork out £2.50 and that despite the fact that the introduction of cheap beet pulp instead of grain has reduced the manufacturing costs even further. But Connemara still produces a nice drop of the stuff. 'It goes down your throat like a torchlight procession', said old Seamus in the shebeen, 'sure, t'is grand altogether.'

'Stand your ground it is too late,
The excise men are at the gate,
Glory be to Paddy but they're drinking it nate,
In the hills of Connemara.'

Note: In November 1977 Gallaher, 'the Hammer', who had been seizing poitin since 1963, retired. Well over 100 raids had yielded thousands of pounds worth of poitin, but even he admitted, 'there are about 200 distilleries in Connemara. What we destroyed was a fraction. I still estimate the industry must be worth one million pounds per year. It won't make any difference if it's legalized, it will continue as an illegal business no matter what.'

The Great Galwally Gang

On December 17th, the RUC, acting on a tip-off raided two houses in Belfast, one in the Galwally area of South Belfast and the other in the markets. There they found two stills, both working full blast, and each turning out 250—300 gallons of poitin wash each week. It was Belfast's biggest haul for 40 years.

Two men were responsible and one of them, Ben Lorimer, tells it as follows:

'I'd been experimenting with making a little poitin ever since, as a teenager I met an old distiller in the Mourne Mountains while I was youth hostelling. Then at Queen's University I met the late and lamented Ken Connell, the historian, and read his essay on the history of illicit distillation. At that time (the 1960s) poitin was being made in the science labs at Queen's but I wasn't really involved in it and I later decided to go into it as a profitable and pleasant experiment. It was pretty easy. I used an old outhouse that had once been a toilet. This had the advantage of already having outlet pipes and drains which took a lot of the smell away.

I used a 10 gallon creamery can as the main unit and a 45 gallon oil drum with a worm in it — though you could use a copper cylinder with a worm in it which you could buy from any plumber or heating engineer. The heat came from a gas cooker although I also used an electric one with a five kilowatt element, which, once it had started I'd knock down to two kilowatts. My recipe was:

25lbs malt.
½lb yeast.
1oz Wine nutrient.

To speed things up you could use 15lbs malt, 10lbs sugar but this wasn't quite as good.

You could use potatoes or any kind of fruit but if you wanted to make it taste like really good whiskey, malt was best. I'd make the mash and let it sit for 14 days to get the best results and then distil it in the normal way. 25lbs of malt gives 12½% alcohol. It would come off at 86% Centigrade and then by the time the temperature crept up to 100%, well of course it was finished and you wouldn't get any more. I would run it three times to bring it up to 85—90% pure alcohol, that is, 150 British proof. Then, using an ordinary hydrometer I'd bring it down to 70 proof by cutting it with water. I added gravy browning — aaah! Bisto! — to colour it.

A ten gallon carboy or can gives you one gallon pure alcohol or 2½ gallons of 70 proof spirit working out at 15 bottles. By the way, for the ten gallon container you had to be sure to use at least a ½ inch or better still a ¾ inch outlet pipe. If you used a narrower pipe it could explode on you as we once found almost to our cost. I used to sell cheaply to a wide range of clubs and pubs all over the town. I charged £6 a gallon — or £1 a bottle when they bought in bulk. A lot did. At the height of it we were selling £400 a week and it cost us just 2/- a bottle to make.

It looked like whiskey and it tasted like whiskey. Publicans and club owners were buying it and putting their own label on it and getting no complaints from the customers. After it was seized they sent samples over to England to be analysed and the forensic report came back said that it had fewer impurities in it than ordinary commercial whiskey. The only ones to suffer were the tax men. Sure the police and the soldiers were amongst by best customers. Why, at one time I had a regular order of a dozen bottles a week for a well known police station in South Belfast.

There were problems of course. For one, neither my partner nor I got much sleep. Some days we'd be working 20 hours a day. I must say about the second still that it differed from the first in that it was made from a five gallon catering pressure cooker with a large Liebig condenser for the worm. It was handier but the recipe was just the same. All you needed was your 70lb drum of malt off a baker and away you went.

Because of a tout we were caught and I had to give it up. We were each fined £200 and got a one year suspended sentence. Pity. Actually, I must confess I didn't completely give it up until two years later to the day, 17th December 1973 we were arrested with a car load of empty bottles in Dublin. Well, there were political protests on that day and the Guards thought that we had the bottles to make petrol bombs or something and of course we couldn't tell them the real reason. Naturally when they raided the house where we were staying they found the still and all the gear. The next day I remember one of them saying angrily to me, "Why the ---- didn't you tell us what you were up to, we'd just have moved you on to someone else's patch." Anyway, it was too late and too many people were involved in it so we were up in court at Howth. The prosecution wanted a £600 fine, but surprisingly, the guards spoke for me and I got off with a £13 fine. That was nice of them, mind you, they got over 8 gallons of the stuff in the house and I was only charged with having two bottles — I wonder whatever happened to the rest....

Of course, with a suspended sentence and a record I can't make it now, still, it was interesting while it lasted.'

In the County Fermanagh

The poitin makers still carry on in Fermanagh. Old W. is still at it somewhere in the hills. He learnt his trade from a County Donegal man and is proud of it. He was caught once by the guards at Ballintra and did six months in Mountjoy but apart from that he hasn't been much bothered. Only a turf fire is good enough for old W. though in an unguarded moment he might confess that Kalor gas is 'rare stuff'.

7lb Baker's yeast
3 stone Brown sugar
4lb treacle
1lb hops

Steep ingredients in 3 gallons of luke warm water at the bottom of a 40 gallon wooden barrel. After steeping fill barrel to ¾ full with cold spring water. Leave in a cool place to settle, preferably buried since it can be noisy. After several weeks transfer to your still, which you seal with Luden — a doughy paste made from oatmeal. A 35 gallon still would produce 16-20 pints this way.

Traditionally a drop of poitin was distilled every Christmas Eve at Buck Island or Breenwe Lough in the past and great care was taken to 'treat the fairies'. This entailed pouring a small libation from *each* run — and it was generally run three times—on to the ground to appease the fairies. W. has a long series of admonitory tales about what would happen if such a precaution wasn't taken — the head might blow off the still, a sudden rainstorm might appear out of a cloudless sky or, worst of all, a phantom peeler would jump out from nowhere and 'grip' you. Better to play safe and give the fairies their due. W. always has and he's lasted a good while!

AN POITIN

'Cumhradh ar a' bpoitín seo—
Is mairg nach nglacann e—
Is iomdha croidhe tartach
　A thóigeann sé.
Chan fhuil ó'n rígh go dtí'n bacach
Nár mhian a bheith 'n-aice,
'S ní'l dhá mhéad a thaithighe
　Nach móide a spéis.'

This is how a Meath poet spoke about poitin. It dates from the mid 19th century and is found in a long out of print collection of folk tales published by the Gaelic League in 1905. The collector was Seosamh Laoide. Tipping's free translation follows:

'Bad cess to this poitin:
Woe to those who don't take it —
Many a thirsty heart
does it lift.
There's none from king to beggar
Who wouldn't like to be near it,
The more he gets used to it
The more he will like it.'

BIBLIOGRAPHY

The best book hitherto to introduce the reader to the history of poitin is Ken Connell's 'Irish Peasant Society' (1968) and it has been of great use to me. What follows is a short list of other useful books or documents on the subject:

Charleton, William
Tales and Stories of the Irish Peasantry, 1846.

Chichester, E
Oppressions and cruelties of Irish Revenue Officers, 1818.

Coyne, WP (Editor)
The distilling industry in Ireland, 1902.

Dorian, Hugh
Donegal sixty years ago. (Manuscript in St. Columb's, Derry.)

Irish Folklore Commission
MS 227. 7th Report of the Commissioners of Excise, 1834.

Londonderry Journal, 1808/14.

Maguire, EB
Irish Whiskey, A history of distilling in Ireland.

Otway, Caesar
A tour in Connaught and Sketches in Ireland, 1839.

Wakefield, E
An account of Ireland, Statistical and Political, 1812.

The Select Committee's Report on Drunkenness in Ireland, 1834.

The Select Committee's Report on Illicit Distillation in Ireland, 1816.

The Select Committee's report on extending the functions of the constabulary in Ireland to the supression or prevention of illicit distillation, 1854.

The Fifth Report of Revenue arising in Ireland, 1823.

There are many books on moonshining in America. Some which I found interesting are:

Baldwin, Leland D
Whiskey Rebels, 1967.

Carr, Jess
The Second Oldest Profession, 1972.

Carson, Gerald
A History of Bourbon, 1972.

Ford, Henry Jones
The Scotch-Irish in America, 1915.

Glasgow, Maude
The Scotch-Irish in Northern Ireland and the American Colonies, 1936.

Wiltse, Henry M.
The Moonshiners, 1895.

Particularly recommended is Joseph Earl Dabney's 'Mountain Spirits'.

There's gold in them there mountains,
There's gold in them there hills,
The natives there are getting it,
By operating stills.

John Judge Jr. 1930